2007

To Brian & Peter

My new very special frien

Enjoy this book wherever. S

NJ or NY think of me.

Can't wait til your return!

Miss ya Merry Christmas

Luv

Terry

MW01687871

Simply Florida

A TASTE OF FLAVORS FROM THE SUNSHINE STATE

FLORIDA EXTENSION ASSOCIATION OF FAMILY AND CONSUMER SCIENCES

Simply Florida

A TASTE OF FLAVORS FROM THE SUNSHINE STATE

Published by Florida Extension Association of Family and Consumer Sciences

Copyright © 2007
Florida Extension Association of Family and Consumer Sciences
University of Florida
P.O. Box 110310
Gainesville, Florida 32611-0310
352-392-1778

Cover photograph© Thomas Wright, UF/IFAS Communications Services
Chicken photograph for Tasty Pork, Poultry & More chapter opener © Stephen Ausmus, ARS/USDA
Selected photographs in the book are a part of the University of Florida/IFAS collection, taken by the following photographers: Thomas Wright, Marisol Amador, Eric Zamora, Milt Putnam, Josh Wickham, and Tara Piasio. The basket artwork and food preparation symbol were contributed by Westshore Jr./Sr. High School graphic arts student Kristen Budesa. The Florida food products and food safety symbols were contributed by Linda Meyers, 4-H program assistant, Okaloosa County, Florida.

This cookbook is a collection of our favorite recipes, which are not necessarily original recipes.

All rights reserved. No part of this publication may be reproduced in any form or by any means, electronic or mechanical, including photocopy and information storage and retrieval systems, without permission in writing from the publisher.

Library of Congress Number: 2006932421
ISBN-10: 0-9787491-0-3
ISBN-13: 978-0-9787491-0-1

Edited and Manufactured by **Favorite Recipes® Press**
An imprint of

FRP™

P.O. Box 305412
Nashville, Tennessee 37230
1-800-358-0560

Art Director: Steve Newman
Book Design: Brad Whitfield and Susan Breining
Project Editor: Tanis Westbrook

Manufactured in the United States of America
First Printing 2007 10,000 copies

Dedication

It is with tremendous gratitude that the Florida Extension Association of Family and Consumer Sciences dedicates this cookbook to the memory of Mary N. Harrison. Professor Harrison was the first Family and Consumer Sciences Extension Specialist at the University of Florida. Throughout her four-decade career as a County Extension Agent and, later, Specialist, Professor Harrison gained national recognition for her educational programs targeting critical issues in consumer education and housing. Most notably, she was a tireless advocate for child passenger safety and seat belt use, development of consumer decision-making skills, and consumer fraud prevention. She remained dedicated to providing training and educational materials to assist Family and Consumer Sciences Extension faculty throughout Florida in educating citizens and enhancing the quality of their lives. Her impact on Extension programming will be felt for years to come.

Table of contents

Symbols are used throughout *Simply Florida* to designate the following:

Florida Food Product

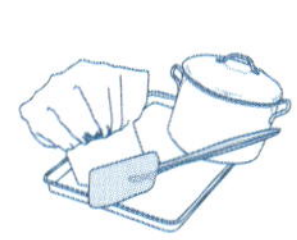

Food Preparation

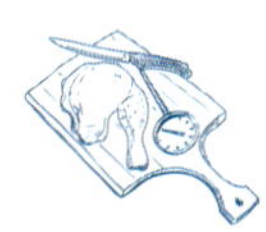

Food Safety

Nutrition and Health

UF UNIVERSITY of FLORIDA
IFAS Extension

Dear Friends:

Simply Florida *is filled with favorite recipes featuring the many tastes of the Sunshine State. Florida agriculture provides the people of Florida, and the world, with nourishing and delicious foods. Today's agriculturists provide consumers with a variety of high quality, safe, healthy, and economical foods. This book highlights many of the products of our state, and provides tips to help you prepare meals that are safe and nutritious.*

As the Dean for Extension of the University of Florida Institute of Food and Agricultural Sciences, I want to congratulate and thank the Extension Family and Consumer Sciences faculty who worked to make this book a reality. Their continued work enriches and improves the lives of Floridians. I also want to thank the commodity groups and organizations that supported this project.

As you browse this book, we hope you will appreciate the many foods of Florida. When you sit down to the table to sample these great recipes, you'll know why our food producers and farm families are simply the best.

Enjoy Simply Florida *and the wonderful foods of Florida agriculture.*

Sincerely,

Larry R. Arrington
Dean for Extension and Director, Florida Cooperative Extension Service

BRAND
BOSS®

Raising Kids

Eating Right

Spending Smart

Living Well

Introduction

Simply Florida: A Taste of Flavors from the Sunshine State is a project of the Florida Extension Association of Family and Consumer Sciences (FEAFCS). FEAFCS is a professional organization educating Florida's Extension Family and Consumer Sciences professionals to empower individuals and families to make informed decisions. Family and Consumer Sciences professionals live and work in Florida's sixty-seven counties and are your neighbors and friends. We serve as an extension of Florida's land grant institutions as employees of the University of Florida Institute of Food and Agricultural Sciences (IFAS) and Florida A&M University, providing information and teaching skills to help people improve their lives.

University of Florida/IFAS Extension is part of the nationwide university-based system integrating agriculture and health and environmental research with higher education and public outreach activities. The Family and Consumer Sciences Educator in your county works to enhance the personal, social, economic, and environmental well-being of individuals and families in your local community.

Research-based educational programs offered throughout the state include:

HEALTH AND NUTRITION

FOOD SAFETY

MONEY MATTERS

HOUSING

AGING AND CAREGIVING

CHILDREN

RELATIONSHIPS

The *Simply Florida* project is a part of our educational programming and is a great resource of information about purchasing and using high-quality, safe Florida commodities. Today's Extension Family and Consumer Sciences professionals continue the tradition and mission of the Cooperative Extension Service to help people help themselves using research, technology, and educational skills of the land grant institutions. Though equipment and techniques have changed, the importance of teaching nutrition, food preparation, safety, and preservation to Florida's families to help maintain good nutrition and healthy families has remained the same.

In 2002, the National Extension Association of Family and Consumer Sciences launched the Living Well public service campaign to raise consumer awareness of the valuable educational resources available through Extension Family and Consumer Sciences. Visit the Living Well Web site at www.learning-andlivingwell.org.

NEAFCS
National Extension Association of Family and Consumer Sciences Florida Affiliate

Sponsors

We appreciate the support of a number of Florida commodity groups which assisted with this project. Their enthusiasm and contributions are evident in the recipes and information presented in this book.

Special recognition goes to the following groups for their monetary support.

Dairy Farmers, Inc.

Florida Extension Association of
Family and Consumer Sciences

University of Florida
IFAS Extension

Florida Tomato Committee

Simply Florida

Flavorful Beef

Flavorful Beef

Beef Rib-Eye Roast with Savory Sauce

2 garlic cloves, minced
1 teaspoon salt
1 teaspoon pepper
1 teaspoon dried thyme leaves
1/2 teaspoon dried tarragon leaves
1 (4-pound) beef rib-eye roast
1/4 cup finely chopped onion
1 cup beef bouillon
2 tablespoons ketchup
1/2 teaspoon sugar

Mix the garlic, salt, pepper, thyme and tarragon in a bowl until of a paste consistency. Spread the garlic mixture evenly over the surface of the roast. Arrange the roast fat side up on a rack in a shallow roasting pan. Insert the bulb of a meat thermometer into the thickest portion of the roast, not resting on fat. Do not add water.

Roast, uncovered, in a preheated 350-degree oven for 18 to 20 minutes per pound or until the meat thermometer registers 145 degrees for rare, or for 20 to 22 minutes per pound or until the meat thermometer registers 160 degrees for medium. Remove the roast to a platter and let stand for 15 to 20 minutes before carving.

Remove the rack from the roasting pan and drain the excess pan drippings. Add the onion to the pan and cook over medium heat for 2 to 3 minutes, stirring constantly. Mix in the bouillon, ketchup and sugar and cook until any brown bits attached to the pan are dissolved, stirring constantly. Increase the heat to medium-high and cook until the liquid is reduced to 3/4 cup. Cut the roast across the grain into 1/2-inch slices and serve with the sauce. *Yield: 14 servings.*

DEGLAZING A PAN

Making a pan sauce is a simple process that produces a rich flavor in just minutes. After sautéing or roasting meat, pour off all but the smallest amount of the pan drippings from the pan. Make sure the pan is hot. Then add wine, stock, or water to the reserved pan drippings and start scraping vigorously with a whisk or wooden spoon while bringing the liquid to a boil. The liquid will reduce in volume to a delicious sauce. The sauce may be enriched by stirring in butter. Serve with the meat as a spoon-on topping.

Chuck Roast Barbecue

1 (2- to 2 1/2-pound) boneless chuck roast, trimmed
2 onions, chopped
3/4 cup cola
1 tablespoon apple cider vinegar
3/4 cup Worcestershire sauce
2 garlic cloves, minced
1 teaspoon beef bouillon granules
1/2 teaspoon dry mustard
1/2 teaspoon chili powder
1/4 teaspoon ground red pepper
1/2 cup ketchup
2 teaspoons butter or margarine
6 hamburger buns

Place the roast and onions in a 4-quart slow cooker. Combine the soda, vinegar, Worcestershire sauce, garlic, bouillon granules, dry mustard, chili powder and red pepper in a bowl and mix well. Reserve 1/2 cup of the soda mixture and store in the refrigerator. Pour the remaining soda mixture over the roast.

Cook, covered, on High for 6 hours; drain. Shred the roast into a heatproof bowl and cover to keep warm.

Combine the reserved soda mixture, ketchup and butter in a small saucepan and cook over medium heat until heated through and of a sauce consistency, stirring constantly. Pour the sauce over the shredded roast and stir gently until coated. Spoon equal amounts of the barbecue onto the buns and serve with potato chips and pickle spears, if desired. *Yield: 6 servings.*

Best Beef Brisket

1 (3- to 5-pound) beef brisket
1/4 cup water
2 tablespoons liquid smoke
2 tablespoons soy sauce
2 teaspoons celery seeds
2 teaspoons pepper
2 teaspoons Worcestershire sauce
1 teaspoon garlic granules
1 teaspoon onion salt

Trim the fat from the brisket and place in a large sealable plastic bag. Mix the water, liquid smoke, soy sauce, celery seeds, pepper, Worcestershire sauce, garlic granules and onion salt in a bowl and pour over the brisket; seal tightly.

Marinate in the refrigerator for 8 to 10 hours, turning occasionally. Remove the brisket from the plastic bag, reserving the marinade. Wrap the undrained brisket in foil and place in a baking pan. Bake in a preheated 300-degree oven for 5 hours or until fork tender. *Yield: 4 servings.*

London Broil

1 (3-pound) lean London broil
3/4 cup soy sauce
1/2 cup lemon juice
3/4 cup sugar
1 small onion, sliced or minced
2 garlic cloves, crushed (optional)
2 teaspoons salt
3/4 teaspoon ground ginger
1/2 teaspoon red food coloring

Arrange the beef fat side up in a shallow dish up to one day in advance. Mix the soy sauce, lemon juice, sugar, onion, garlic, salt, ginger and food coloring in a bowl and pour over the beef. Marinate, covered, in the refrigerator, turning occasionally.

Drain the beef approximately 3 1/2 hours before serving, reserving the marinade. Roll the beef and tie securely with kitchen string. Arrange the roll on a rack in a shallow roasting pan and insert a meat thermometer into the center of the meaty portion. Roast in a preheated 350-degree oven for 3 hours or until the meat thermometer registers 145 degrees for rare or 160 degrees for medium, basting several times with the reserved marinade. Cut into 1/4-inch slices. *Yield: 6 servings.*

Lime-Marinated Steak

- $^1/_2$ cup fresh lime juice
- 2 tablespoons vegetable oil
- $^1/_2$ teaspoon hot red pepper sauce
- $^1/_2$ teaspoon garlic pepper
- 1 (16- to 18-ounce) boneless top round steak
- 2 teaspoons freshly ground pepper

Mix the lime juice, oil, hot sauce and garlic pepper in a large shallow dish. Trim the visible fat from the steak and arrange the steak in the lime juice mixture, turning to coat. Marinate, covered, in the refrigerator for 6 to 8 hours, turning occasionally. Remove the steak from the marinade, discarding the marinade. Sprinkle the steak with the pepper and grill or broil for 3 to 4 minutes per side or to the desired degree of doneness. Remove the steak to a cutting board and cut across the grain into thin slices. Garnish with lime wedges. *Yield: 4 servings.*

Pepper Steak

- 1 to $1^1/_2$ pounds beef round steak
- 1 tablespoon vegetable oil
- 1 garlic clove, crushed or finely chopped
- $^1/_2$ teaspoon sliced spiced ginger, or $^1/_4$ teaspoon ground ginger
- 2 teaspoons cornstarch
- 2 tablespoons soy sauce
- $^1/_2$ cup water
- 1 teaspoon instant beef bouillon
- $^1/_4$ teaspoon pepper
- 2 cups (1-inch) pieces green bell pepper
- 1 onion, thinly sliced
- 2 large ribs celery, diagonally sliced, or 1 teaspoon celery seeds
- 1 (2-ounce) jar chopped pimento (optional)

Cut the steak into strips, $^1/_2$ inch wide and $1^1/_2$ inches long. Toss the steak with the oil in a microwave-safe dish. Microwave on High for 2 to 3 minutes or until the steak is brown, stirring after 1 minute. Stir in the garlic and ginger and microwave, covered, for 7 minutes.

Dissolve the cornstarch in the soy sauce in a bowl. Stir the cornstarch mixture, water, bouillon and pepper into the steak mixture. Add the bell pepper, onion, celery and pimento and mix well. Microwave, covered, on Medium for 7 to 10 minutes or until the vegetables are tender-crisp. *Yield: 4 servings.*

All-Day Slow-Cooker Beef

1 onion, sliced and separated into rings
3 large carrots, chopped
2 large ribs celery, chopped
1 green bell pepper, thinly sliced
1 1/2 pounds beef stew meat, or any cut of beef roast
2 tablespoons vegetable oil
1/2 envelope onion soup mix
1/2 teaspoon freshly ground pepper
2 garlic cloves, minced
1/2 cup water
1/2 cup tomato juice
2 teaspoons Worcestershire sauce
1 teaspoon steak sauce

Place the onion, carrots, celery and bell pepper in a slow cooker. Cut the beef into bite-size portions. Heat the oil in a large skillet and add the beef. Cook until brown on all sides. Sprinkle the beef with the soup mix, pepper and garlic and arrange over the vegetables.

Mix the water, tomato juice, Worcestershire sauce and steak sauce in a bowl and pour over the prepared layers. Turn the slow cooker on High and cook for 30 minutes. Reduce the heat to Low and cook, covered, for 7 to 9 hours or to the desired consistency. *Yield: 8 servings.*

NOTE: To freeze, cut and brown the beef as directed above. Let stand until cool. Place the browned beef in a large sealable freezer bag and top with the remaining ingredients; seal tightly. Label the bag and freeze for up to six months. The day before serving, remove the bag from the freezer and thaw in the refrigerator for 8 to 10 hours. Place the contents of the freezer bag in a slow cooker and cook as directed above.

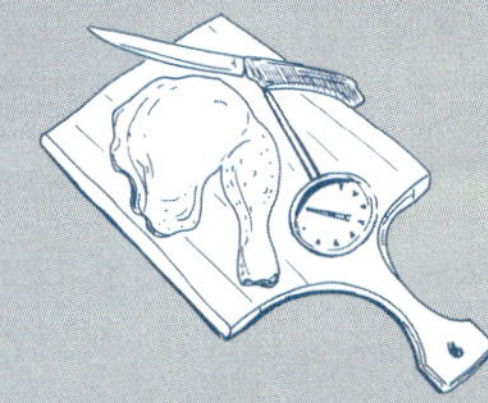

CLEANING CUTTING BOARDS

To keep cutting boards clean, wash with hot, soapy water after each use; then rinse with clean water and air dry or pat dry with clean paper towels. Nonporous acrylic boards, plastic boards, glass boards, or solid wood boards can be washed in a dishwasher. Be aware that laminated boards may crack and split.

Both wooden and plastic cutting boards can be sanitized with a solution of one teaspoon liquid chlorine bleach per quart of water. Flood the surface of the cutting board with the bleach solution and let stand for several minutes. Rinse with clean water and air dry or pat dry. Discard cutting boards that become excessively worn or develop hard-to-clean grooves.

Beef Stroganoff

12 ounces egg noodles or fettuccini
2 tablespoons butter
1 pound beef stew meat, cut into bite-size pieces
8 ounces mushrooms, trimmed
1/2 onion, chopped
1 teaspoon salt
1/4 teaspoon pepper
2 tablespoons butter
3 tablespoons all-purpose flour
1 cup beef broth
1 cup sour cream

Cook the pasta using the package directions; drain. Cover to keep warm. Melt 2 tablespoons butter in a 12-inch skillet and add the beef, mushrooms, onion, salt and pepper. Cook until the beef is cooked through, stirring frequently. Remove the beef and mushrooms to a bowl, reserving the pan drippings.

Mix the butter and flour with the reserved pan drippings. Stir in the broth, sour cream, beef and mushrooms. Cook just until heated through, stirring frequently; do not boil. Spoon the beef mixture over the hot pasta on a serving platter and serve immediately. *Yield: 6 servings.*

Polish Delight

1 pound hot bulk pork sausage
1 pound lean ground beef (90/10)
1 pound processed cheese, cubed
2 teaspoons Worcestershire sauce
1 teaspoon oregano
1/2 teaspoon garlic powder
2 loaves party rye bread

Brown the sausage in a skillet, stirring until crumbly. Drain and blot dry with paper towels. Brown the ground beef in a skillet, stirring until crumbly; drain. Combine the sausage, ground beef, cheese, Worcestershire sauce, oregano and garlic powder in a skillet and mix well. Cook over low heat until the cheese melts, stirring frequently. Spread the beef mixture on the slices of party rye and arrange the slices in a single layer on a baking sheet. Bake in a preheated 350-degree oven for 15 minutes. Serve immediately. *Yield: 10 servings.*

NOTE: These may be frozen for up to three months. Freeze on a baking sheet until firm and transfer to a sealable freezer bag; freeze. Remove the desired amount as needed and bake as directed above.

Chili Cheese Tater Tot Casserole

2 pounds lean ground beef
1 onion, chopped
2 (15-ounce) cans chili beans
1 (12-ounce) can petite diced tomatoes
1 (11-ounce) can whole kernel corn, drained and rinsed
1 (8-ounce) package shredded reduced-fat Colby and
    Monterey Jack cheese blend
1 (32-ounce) package frozen Tater Tots
1/4 cup pickled sliced jalapeño chiles, or
    2 fresh jalapeño chiles, sliced (optional)

Brown the ground beef with the onion in large skillet over medium-high heat, stirring until the ground beef is crumbly and the onion is tender; drain. Stir in the beans, undrained tomatoes and corn.

Spoon the ground beef mixture into a lightly greased 9×13-inch baking pan and sprinkle with the cheese. Top with the Tater Tots. Bake in a preheated 350-degree oven for 1 hour or until the Tater Tots are golden brown. Sprinkle with the jalapeño chiles and serve immediately. *Yield: 8 servings.*

Lentil Beef Casserole

2 cups dried lentils
5 cups water
2 teaspoons salt
1 pound ground beef
1 envelope onion soup mix
1 cup ketchup
1 teaspoon prepared mustard
1 teaspoon vinegar
1 cup water

Combine the lentils, 5 cups water and the salt in a saucepan and bring to a gentle boil. Boil gently for 20 to 30 minutes or until the lentils are tender; drain.

Brown the ground beef in a skillet, stirring until crumbly; drain. Stir in the lentils, soup mix, ketchup, prepared mustard, vinegar and 1 cup water. Pour the lentil mixture into a 2-quart baking dish and bake in a preheated 400-degree oven for 30 minutes. One cup dried lentils equals two cups cooked lentils. *Yield: 4 servings.*

Mexican Beef and Rice

1 pound ground chuck
2 bell peppers, chopped
1 (10-ounce) package frozen white kernel corn
1 (14-ounce) can diced tomatoes with green chiles
1 (6-ounce) can reduced-salt tomato juice
1 cup water
1/2 teaspoon chili powder
1/4 teaspoon dried whole oregano
1/4 teaspoon salt
1/4 teaspoon freshly ground pepper
1 garlic clove, minced
1 3/4 cups instant rice
1 cup (4 ounces) shredded Cheddar cheese or Mexican blend cheese

Brown the ground chuck in a large skillet over medium heat, stirring until crumbly. Drain and wipe the excess pan drippings from the skillet. Return the ground chuck to the skillet and stir in the bell peppers, corn, tomatoes with green chiles, tomato juice, water, chili powder, oregano, salt, pepper and garlic.

Bring to a boil and stir in the rice. Remove from the heat and let stand, covered, for 5 minutes. If the beef mixture is too soupy, return the saucepan to the heat and cook until of the desired consistency. Fluff with a fork and sprinkle with the cheese. Let stand, covered, for 2 minutes or until the cheese melts. *Yield: 6 servings.*

SHEPHERD'S PIE

1 pound ground beef
1/2 cup chopped celery
2 tablespoons chopped onion
2 tablespoons all-purpose flour
1 cup milk
3/4 cup beef broth
1 teaspoon pepper
1 (10-ounce) package frozen mixed vegetables, cooked and drained
2 cups prepared mashed potatoes
1/4 cup (1 ounce) shredded sharp processed American cheese

Brown the ground beef with the celery and onion in a 10-inch skillet, stirring until the ground beef is crumbly and the vegetables are tender; drain. Add the flour and stir until combined. Stir in the milk and broth. Bring to a boil and cook until thickened, stirring constantly. Stir in the pepper and mixed vegetables.

Spoon the ground beef mixture into a 9×13-inch baking dish and spread with the mashed potatoes. Bake in a preheated 400-degree oven for 20 to 25 minutes or until the mashed potatoes are brown. Sprinkle with the cheese and serve immediately. *Yield: 4 servings.*

SPAGHETTI PIE

7 ounces thin spaghetti, cooked and drained
2 tablespoons margarine
1/4 cup (1 ounce) grated Parmesan cheese
2 eggs, lightly beaten
2 cups cottage cheese
1 pound lean ground beef
1 pound bulk pork sausage
1 (8-ounce) jar spaghetti sauce
8 ounces mozzarella cheese, shredded

Toss the pasta, margarine, Parmesan cheese and eggs in a bowl. Pat the pasta mixture over the bottom and up the side of a 10-inch pie plate or large quiche pan. Spread the cottage cheese over the prepared layer. Brown the ground beef and sausage in a 10-inch skillet, stirring until crumby; drain. Stir in the spaghetti sauce and cook until heated through, stirring occasionally. Spoon the ground beef mixture over the cottage cheese and bake in a preheated 350-degree oven for 30 minutes. Sprinkle with the mozzarella cheese and bake for 5 minutes longer. Cut into wedges and serve immediately. *Yield: 6 servings.*

Inside-Out Ravioli

16 ounces medium pasta shells
2 (10-ounce) packages frozen chopped spinach
2 pounds lean ground chuck
2 onions, chopped
1/2 teaspoon garlic powder
1 (32-ounce) jar spaghetti sauce with mushrooms
1 (12-ounce) can tomato paste
1 large can mushrooms (optional)
1 teaspoon salt
1/2 teaspoon pepper
8 ounces Cheddar cheese, shredded
1 cup cottage cheese
1 cup fine dry bread crumbs
4 eggs, beaten
1/2 cup vegetable oil
1 cup (4 ounces) grated Parmesan cheese, Romano cheese, Cheddar cheese, or cheese of choice

Cook the pasta using the package directions and drain. Cook the spinach using the package directions. Drain, reserving 2 cups of the cooking liquid.

Brown the ground chuck with the onions in a skillet, stirring until the ground chuck is crumbly and the onions are tender; drain. Stir in the garlic powder. Add the reserved spinach cooking liquid, spaghetti sauce, tomato paste, mushrooms, salt and pepper and mix well.

Mix the pasta and spinach in a bowl. Stir in the Cheddar cheese, cottage cheese, bread crumbs, eggs and oil. Pat the pasta mixture over the bottom of a 12×12-inch lasagna pan or two 9×12-inch baking pans. Spoon the ground chuck mixture over the prepared layer and sprinkle with the Parmesan cheese. Bake in a preheated 350-degree oven for 30 to 40 minutes or until bubbly. Let stand for 10 minutes before serving. *Yield: 14 servings.*

NOTE: You may prepare up to one day in advance and store, covered, in the refrigerator. Bake just before serving.

STUFFED CABBAGE

$^1/_3$ cup rice
$1^1/_2$ pounds ground beef
$^1/_2$ small onion, chopped
2 eggs, lightly beaten
Salt and pepper to taste
2 cups water
1 head cabbage, trimmed and separated into leaves
1 cup water
$^1/_4$ cup vinegar
1 (16-ounce) can tomatoes
2 teaspoons sugar

Parboil the rice in a saucepan and drain. Combine the rice, ground beef, onion, eggs, salt and pepper in a bowl and mix well. Bring 2 cups water to a boil in a saucepan and add the cabbage leaves. Boil for several minutes or just until softened; drain.

Line a medium saucepan with some of the cabbage leaves. Fill each of the remaining cabbage leaves with a spoonful of the ground beef mixture and roll to enclose the filling. Arrange the cabbage rolls in the cabbage-lined saucepan and add 1 cup water and the vinegar. Mix the undrained tomatoes and sugar in a bowl. Season to taste with salt and pepper and pour the tomato mixture over the cabbage rolls. Cook, covered, over low heat for $2^1/_2$ hours. *Yield: 8 servings.*

HERB SHAKERS

Herb Shakers make novel gifts for holidays or birthdays and they are a good way to introduce a health-conscious friend to alternative seasonings for salt. Both of these Herb Shakers can be used for meats, seafood, soups, stews, and vegetables. Just blend, store in a shaker, and serve.

For ***Bountiful Bouquet Mix****, blend 2 teaspoons thyme, 2 teaspoons marjoram, 1 1/2 teaspoons ground rosemary, 1 teaspoon ground sage and 1 teaspoon sweet basil and pour into a shaker.*

For ***Zesty Herb Mix****, blend 1 1/2 teaspoons savory, 1 1/2 teaspoons marjoram, 1 teaspoon thyme, 1 teaspoon ground sage, 1 teaspoon ground rosemary and 1 teaspoon tarragon and pour into a shaker.*

Stuffed Green Peppers

- 4 large green bell peppers
- 1 1/2 pounds lean ground beef
- 2/3 cup chopped onion
- 1 (14-ounce) can chopped tomatoes
- 2/3 cup long grain rice
- 1/2 cup water
- 2 tablespoons Worcestershire sauce
- 1 teaspoon crushed dried oregano or basil
- 1/4 teaspoon pepper
- 1 cup (4 ounces) shredded mozzarella cheese

Cut the bell peppers lengthwise into halves. Remove the stem ends, seeds and membranes. Immerse the bell peppers in boiling water for 3 minutes and drain. Invert onto paper towels to drain completely.

Brown the ground beef with the onion in a skillet, stirring until the ground beef is crumbly and the onion is tender; drain. Stir in the undrained tomatoes, rice, 1/2 cup water, the Worcestershire sauce, oregano and pepper. Bring to a boil over high heat and reduce the heat to low.

Simmer, covered, for 15 to 18 minutes or until the rice is tender, stirring occasionally. Remove from the heat and stir in 1/2 cup of the cheese. Mound the ground beef mixture in the bell pepper halves and arrange in a single layer in an 8×8-inch baking dish, surrounding the bell peppers with the remaining ground beef mixture. Bake in a preheated 375-degree oven for 15 minutes or until heated through. Sprinkle with the remaining 1/2 cup cheese and let stand for 1 to 2 minutes before serving. *Yield: 8 servings.*

UPSIDE-DOWN PIZZA CASSEROLE

2 pounds ground beef
2 onions, chopped
1/2 cup chopped bell pepper
1 tablespoon dried Italian seasoning
1/4 cup all-purpose flour
1 (26-ounce) jar tomato pasta sauce, flavor of choice
1 teaspoon vegetable oil
1 1/2 cups (6 ounces) shredded mozzarella cheese
1 (13-ounce) can refrigerator pizza crust
1 tablespoon olive oil
1/2 cup (2 ounces) shredded mozzarella cheese
2 tablespoons grated Parmesan cheese
1 teaspoon dried Italian seasoning

Brown the ground beef with the onions, bell pepper and 1 tablespoon Italian seasoning in a large skillet, stirring until the ground beef is crumbly and the vegetables are tender; drain. Add the flour and stir until combined. Stir in the pasta sauce and bring to a boil, stirring constantly. Immediately remove from the heat.

Coat a 9×13-inch baking dish with the vegetable oil and spoon the ground beef mixture into the prepared baking dish. Sprinkle with 1 1/2 cups mozzarella cheese. Unroll the pizza crust and place over the prepared layers, tucking the edges of the crust into the baking dish if necessary. Brush the crust with the olive oil and sprinkle with 1/2 cup mozzarella cheese, the Parmesan cheese and 1 teaspoon Italian seasoning. Bake in a preheated 425-degree oven for 15 to 20 minutes or until golden brown. *Yield: 6 servings.*

Chili

1 pound bacon
3 small or medium onions, chopped
3 pounds ground beef
3 (16-ounce) cans kidney beans, mashed or puréed in food processor
3 (15-ounce) cans stewed tomatoes, crushed
2 envelopes chili seasoning mix
$1^1/2$ teaspoons seasoned salt
1 teaspoon (or less) pepper
1 teaspoon chili powder
$1^1/2$ to 2 cups water used to rinse out cans

Cook the bacon in a skillet until brown and crisp. Drain, reserving the bacon drippings. Crumble the bacon. Cook the onions in the reserved bacon drippings until tender; drain. Brown the ground beef in a skillet, stirring until crumbly; drain.

Combine the beans, tomatoes, seasoning mix, seasoned salt, pepper, chili powder and water in a stockpot. Add the bacon, onions and ground beef and mix well. Simmer until thickened and heated through, stirring occasionally. Ladle into chili bowls. Serve over hot cooked rice, if desired. *Yield: 30 servings.*

Taco Soup

1 pound ground beef
1 large onion, chopped
3 (16-ounce) cans Mexican-style chili beans
$1^1/2$ cups water
1 (4-ounce) can chopped green chiles
1 envelope taco seasoning mix
1 envelope ranch salad dressing mix

Brown the ground beef with the onion in a large saucepan, stirring until the ground beef is crumbly and the onion is tender; drain. Stir in the undrained beans, water, green chiles, taco seasoning mix and salad dressing mix.

Bring to a simmer and simmer for 15 minutes, stirring occasionally. Ladle into soup bowls and serve with tortilla chips or corn chips. You may freeze for up to 3 months. *Yield: 12 servings.*

Pepper Pot Soup

8 ounces corned beef
8 ounces round steak, fat trimmed
1 tablespoon butter or margarine
2 quarts water
1 cup all-purpose flour
1 tablespoon nonfat dry milk powder
1/8 teaspoon salt
6 okra pods, chopped
8 ounces shrimp, peeled and deveined (optional)
1 pound yams, peeled and chopped
1 pound callalu or spinach, trimmed
1 small onion, chopped
1 scallion, chopped
1 sprig of thyme

Soak the corned beef in water for 30 minutes and drain. Cut the corned beef and round steak into bite-size pieces. Melt the margarine in a stockpot and add the corned beef and round steak. Sauté until brown. Add 2 cups of the water and cook, covered, for 20 minutes.

Mix the flour, milk powder and salt in a bowl. Add enough of the remaining water to make a soft dough and mix well. Add the remaining water to the beef mixture and bring to a boil. Stir in the okra, shrimp, yams, callalu, onion, scallion and thyme.

Drop the dough by teaspoonfuls into the soup mixture. Simmer for 30 to 40 minutes or until of the desired consistency, stirring occasionally. Ladle into soup bowls. *Yield: 6 servings.*

NOTE: Callalu or callaloo, a leafy green vegetable similar to spinach, has a high iron, calcium, and vitamin A content. It is the most versatile and widely used green leafy vegetable in Jamaica. Rinse with water and strip the stems leaving the flowering shoots and leaves intact. Finely chop or cut into bite-size pieces.

Taco Salad

8 ounces 93% lean ground beef
1/2 onion, chopped
1/2 teaspoon chili powder
1/2 teaspoon ground cumin
4 cups chopped iceberg lettuce
1/2 cup canned kidney beans, drained and rinsed
1 fully ripened fresh Florida tomato, chopped
1/2 cup canned whole kernel corn, drained and rinsed
1 cup nacho cheese tortilla chips, crushed
1/2 cup reduced-fat French or Catalina salad dressing (optional)

Brown the ground beef with the onion, chili powder and ground cumin in a skillet sprayed with nonstick cooking spray, stirring until the ground beef is crumbly and the onion is tender; drain. Toss the ground beef mixture, lettuce, beans, tomato, corn, chips and salad dressing in a bowl until combined. Serve immediately. *Yield: 8 servings.*

Chili Sauce for Hot Dogs

2 pounds ground beef or ground turkey
3 large onions, chopped
1 1/2 teaspoons cayenne pepper
1 1/2 ounces chili powder
1 quart water
1 (32-ounce) bottle ketchup
2 (14-ounce) cans tomato purée

Combine the ground beef, onions, cayenne pepper, chili powder and water in a large saucepan and mix well. Simmer until the liquid is reduced by half, stirring occasionally.

Stir the ketchup and tomato purée into the ground beef mixture and cook until heated through. Serve over hot dogs with additional chopped onion. *Yield: 20 servings.*

Tasty Pork, Poultry & More

Tasty Pork, Poultry & More

Pork Tenderloin

- 2 (1 1/2- to 2-pound) pork tenderloins
- 1/3 cup olive oil
- 1/4 cup orange, apricot or kumquat preserves
- 2 garlic cloves, minced
- Juice of 1 lemon
- 1 teaspoon grated fresh ginger
- 1/2 teaspoon salt
- 1/2 teaspoon pepper
- 1/3 cup sliced almonds
- 1 tablespoon olive oil
- 3/4 cup orange juice
- 1/2 cup orange, apricot or kumquat preserves
- Grated zest of 8 kumquats
- 1 tablespoon minced crystallized ginger
- 8 ounces sugar snap peas, blanched and drained
- Carrot slivers to taste

Arrange the tenderloins in a large shallow dish. Mix 1/3 cup olive oil, 1/4 cup preserves, the garlic, lemon juice, fresh ginger, salt and pepper in a bowl and pour over the tenderloins, turning to coat. Marinate, covered, in the refrigerator for 2 to 10 hours, turning occasionally.

Spread the almonds on a baking sheet and toast in a preheated 300-degree oven for 10 minutes or until light brown, stirring occasionally. Remove the almonds from the oven and let cool. Increase the oven temperature to 450 degrees.

Drain the tenderloins, discarding the marinade. Brown the tenderloins on all sides in 1 tablespoon olive in a large cast-iron skillet. Roast in the oven for 15 minutes or until a meat thermometer registers 160 degrees for medium or 170 degrees for well done. Remove the tenderloins to a cutting board, reserving the pan drippings.

Scrape the bottom of the skillet to dislodge any brown bits and stir the orange juice, 1/2 cup preserves, the kumquat zest and crystallized ginger into the reserved pan drippings. Cook until the liquid is reduced by half and of a sauce consistency, stirring constantly. Remove from the heat.

Slice the tenderloins and arrange the slices on a serving platter. Surround with the sugar snap peas and drizzle with the kumquat ginger sauce over all. Sprinkle with the almonds and carrot slivers. *Yield: 8 servings.*

The nutritional profile includes the entire amount of the marinade.

Herbed Pork Roast

$2^1/2$ teaspoons salt
1 teaspoon thyme leaves
1 teaspoon pepper
$^1/2$ teaspoon ground nutmeg
1 (4- to 6-pound) pork loin
2 onions, chopped
2 small carrots, chopped
4 or 5 celery leaves, chopped
3 or 4 sprigs of parsley, chopped
2 large garlic cloves, minced
1 (10-ounce) can chicken broth
3 bay leaves
4 whole cloves
2 to 3 tablespoons self-rising flour

Mix the salt, thyme, pepper and nutmeg in a bowl. Rub the surface of the pork with the salt mixture. Arrange the pork in a roasting pan and roast in a preheated 450-degree oven for 30 minutes. Reduce the oven temperature to 350 degrees.

Add the onions, carrots, celery leaves, parsley, garlic, broth, bay leaves and cloves to the roasting pan and roast, covered, until a meat thermometer inserted in the middle of the pork registers 160 degrees, basting frequently with the pan juices. Remove the pork to a heated platter, reserving the pan juices.

Discard the bay leaves and cloves and skim the fat from the reserved pan juices. Press the pan juices and vegetables through a sieve or process in a blender until puréed. Return the purée to the roasting pan and whisk in the self-rising flour until blended. Cook until thick and bubbly and of a gravy consistency, stirring constantly. Serve the gravy with the pork. *Yield: 8 servings.*

Pork Casserole Milano

2 tablespoons vegetable oil
1 pound boneless pork, cut into 1-inch strips
1 green bell pepper, chopped
1/2 cup chopped onion
1/2 cup chopped celery
1 (3-ounce) can sliced mushrooms
1 teaspoon Worcestershire sauce
1 teaspoon salt
1/8 teaspoon pepper
1/2 teaspoon dried basil leaves
1 (10-ounce) can cream of mushroom soup
1/2 cup milk
3 quarts water
8 ounces spaghetti
1 fully ripened fresh Florida tomato,
peeled and thinly sliced
1 1/2 cups croutons
2 tablespoons butter, melted
1 cup (4 ounces) shredded Cheddar cheese

Heat the oil in a large skillet and add the pork. Cook until the pork is brown on all sides and stir in the bell pepper, onion and celery. Sauté until the vegetables are tender. Add the undrained mushrooms, Worcestershire sauce, salt, pepper and basil and simmer, covered, for 25 minutes, stirring occasionally. Stir in the soup and milk and simmer, covered, for 5 minutes longer.

Bring the water to a boil in a stockpot and add the pasta. Cook for 8 minutes and drain. Toss the pasta with the pork mixture in a bowl and spoon into a 2-quart baking dish. Overlap the tomato slices around the edge of the baking dish. Toss the croutons with the butter in a bowl and sprinkle the croutons over the tomatoes.

Bake in a preheated 350-degree oven for 20 minutes. Sprinkle the cheese over the croutons and bake for 10 minutes longer or until the cheese melts.
Yield: 8 servings.

STUFFING A PORK CHOP

Adding a savory stuffing to pork chops makes them a dish fit for company. Select at least 1-inch-thick chops. Using a paring knife, make a 1-inch cut horizontally into the long side of the pork chop. Wiggle the knife back and forth to make a small opening. Remove the knife, turn it over so the serrated edge of the blade faces in the opposite direction and again wiggle the knife back and forth. Spoon your favorite stuffing into the pocket. Brown the chops in an ovenproof skillet and then transfer the skillet to the oven to complete the cooking process; the chops should register 160 degrees on a meat thermometer when done.

Suwannee County Pork Chops

3 tablespoons vegetable oil
5 (8-ounce) center-cut pork chops, 1 inch thick
1 onion, chopped
1 (14-ounce) can diced tomatoes
1 (10-ounce) can tomato sauce with green chiles
1 cup water
1/2 teaspoon salt
1/2 teaspoon pepper

Heat the oil in a large skillet and add the pork chops. Cook until brown on both sides and stir in the onion. Cook for 2 minutes, stirring frequently. Add the undrained tomatoes, tomato sauce, water, salt and pepper and mix well. Simmer, covered, over low heat for 1 1/2 hours or until the chops register 160 degrees on a meat thermometer and the sauce is thickened, stirring occasionally. *Yield: 5 servings.*

Down South Barbecue

2 onions, sliced
4- to 5-pounds pork shoulder or beef, cut into pieces (bone-in pieces may be used)
2 cups water
5 or 6 whole cloves
1 (16-ounce) bottle barbecue sauce
1 onion, chopped

Arrange half the onion slices in the bottom of a slow cooker and top with the pork. Cover with the remaining onion slices. Add the water and cloves and cook, covered, on Low for 8 to 12 hours or until the pork is fork tender.

Remove and discard the bones and fat from the pork and return the pork to the slow cooker. Add the barbecue sauce and chopped onion to the pork and mix well. Cook, covered, on High for 1 to 3 hours or on Low for 4 to 8 hours or until of the desired consistency and flavor, stirring two or three times during the cooking process. Serve on buns. *Yield: 6 servings.*

Kumquat Chicken

1 (6-pound) chicken
1 tablespoon olive oil
Salt and pepper to taste
1 teaspoon dried sage
1 teaspoon dried thyme
15 kumquats, cut crosswise into halves and seeded
20 unpeeled garlic cloves
$1^{1}/_{4}$ cups chicken broth
1 cup dry white wine
$^{1}/_{2}$ cup kumquat marmalade

Rub the outside surface of the chicken with the olive oil. Sprinkle salt and pepper over the outside surface and inside cavity. Rub the sage and thyme over the outside surface and inside cavity. Arrange the chicken in a deep 10×13-inch baking dish. Fill the inside cavity with the kumquats. Place the garlic cloves around the chicken and pour the broth and wine into the baking dish.

Bake, covered, in a preheated 375-degree oven for 1 to $1^{1}/_{2}$ hours or until the chicken is brown and cooked through. Remove the chicken to a platter, reserving $1^{1}/_{2}$ cups of the pan juices. Remove the kumquats and garlic to bowl. The garlic is great for spreading on bread.

Pour the reserved $1^{1}/_{2}$ cups pan juices into a 2-quart saucepan. Cook until the liquid is reduced to 1 cup. Stir in the marmalade and cook until thick and of a glaze consistency, stirring constantly. Pour the glaze over the chicken. Garnish with some of the reserved kumquats and the roasted garlic, if desired. *Yield: 8 servings.*

Beef Baked Chicken

If you have never tried this, do so. It is wonderful.

1 (4-ounce) package dried beef
6 (4-ounce) boneless skinless chicken breast fillets
3 slices bacon, cut into halves
1 (10-ounce) can cream of mushroom soup
1 cup sour cream

Rinse the dried beef with water to remove the salt and pat dry. Arrange the dried beef over the bottom of a 9×13-inch baking dish. Place the chicken in a single layer over the beef and top each chicken breast with a half slice bacon.

Bake in a preheated 350-degree oven for 30 minutes. Mix the soup and sour cream in a saucepan and cook over low heat until blended, stirring occasionally. Pour the soup mixture over the chicken and bake for 45 to 60 minutes longer or until the chicken is cooked through. *Yield: 6 servings.*

Cheesy Baked Chicken

4 (4-ounce) chicken breast fillets
4 slices Swiss cheese
1 (10-ounce) can reduced-sodium cream of chicken soup
1/2 cup fat-free milk
1/2 cup nonfat sour cream
1 1/2 cups herb-seasoned stuffing mix

Arrange the chicken in a single layer in a shallow baking dish. Top each chicken breast with a slice of cheese. Mix the soup, milk and sour cream in a bowl and pour over the chicken. Top with the stuffing mix.

Bake, covered with foil, in a preheated 350-degree oven for 45 minutes. Remove the foil and bake for 15 minutes longer or until the chicken is cooked through and golden brown. *Yield: 4 servings.*

Oven-Fried Mexican Chicken

1 cup low-sodium vegetable juice cocktail
1/4 teaspoon hot red pepper sauce
2 1/4 pounds chicken pieces, skinned
2 ounces sharp Cheddar cheese, shredded
1 1/2 cups cornflake crumbs
1 teaspoon garlic powder
1/2 teaspoon salt
1/2 teaspoon pepper
1/2 teaspoon chili powder
1/2 teaspoon paprika
1/2 teaspoon oregano leaves
1/2 teaspoon ground cumin

Mix the vegetable juice cocktail and hot sauce in a shallow dish and add the chicken, turning to coat. Marinate at room temperature for 30 minutes, or cover and marinate in the refrigerator for 3 hours, turning frequently. Drain, discarding the marinade.

Mix the cheese, cornflake crumbs, garlic powder, salt, pepper, chili powder, paprika, oregano and cumin in a sealable plastic bag. Add the chicken in batches and shake to coat. Arrange the coated chicken in a single layer on a baking sheet sprayed with nonstick cooking spray. Sprinkle the chicken with any remaining crumb mixture and press lightly to adhere. Bake in a preheated 375-degree oven for 1 hour or until the chicken is cooked through and crisp. *Yield: 8 servings.*

NOTE: The cooking time is reduced by 20 to 30 minutes if using boneless chicken pieces.

The nutritional profile includes the entire amount of the marinade.

HERB SHAKER FOR CHICKEN

*For **Hot Spicy Mix**, process 1/4 cup dried minced onion, 1 tablespoon sweet basil, 1 tablespoon ground cumin, 1 tablespoon garlic powder and 1 tablespoon cracked pepper in a blender at high speed for one minute or until of a powdery consistency. Pour into a shaker. Use on baked chicken or as a spicy dash to fried chicken. It is also tasty on meat, fish, or vegetables.*

Oven-Fried Chicken

$1/3$ cup all-purpose flour
$1\,1/2$ teaspoons salt
1 teaspoon paprika
$1/4$ teaspoon poultry seasoning
$1/8$ teaspoon pepper
1 ($2\,1/2$- to $3\,1/2$-pound) chicken, cut up
$1/4$ cup ($1/2$ stick) butter
1 cup rice
$1/2$ cup chopped green bell pepper
$1/2$ cup chopped onion
$1\,1/2$ teaspoons salt
Pepper to taste
3 cups chicken broth, heated
2 large fully ripened fresh Florida tomatoes, cut into wedges

Sift the flour, $1\,1/2$ teaspoons salt, the paprika, poultry seasoning and $1/8$ teaspoon pepper into a nonrecycled brown paper bag. Add the chicken one piece at a time and shake to thoroughly coat. Melt the butter in a baking pan in a preheated 400-degree oven. Remove the chicken from the bag and arrange skin side down in the butter.

Bake for 25 minutes. Remove the chicken to a platter, reserving the pan drippings. Add the rice, bell pepper and onion to the reserved pan drippings and season the rice mixture with the $1\,1/2$ teaspoons salt and pepper. Arrange the chicken over the rice mixture skin side up. Pour the hot broth over the rice mixture, making sure all the rice mixture is covered by the broth. Arrange the tomato wedges over the chicken. Bake for 45 minutes longer or until the rice is tender and the chicken is cooked through, adding additional broth or water if the rice becomes too dry. *Yield: 6 servings.*

Chicken Fantastic

4 (4-ounce) chicken breast fillets
1 (8-ounce) jar apricot preserves
1 (8-ounce) bottle Russian salad dressing
1 envelope onion soup mix

Arrange the chicken in a single layer in a 9×13-inch baking dish. Mix the preserves, salad dressing and soup mix in a bowl and spoon the preserve mixture over the chicken. Bake, covered with foil, in a preheated 350-degree oven for 1 hour or until cooked through. *Yield: 4 servings.*

Linda's Favorite Chicken

1 teaspoon vegetable oil
1/2 cup chopped onion
1/2 cup ketchup
1/2 cup water
2 tablespoons brown sugar
1 1/2 teaspoons Worcestershire sauce
2 tablespoons white vinegar
1/2 teaspoon chili powder
1/4 teaspoon crushed celery seeds
1 (3-pound) chicken, cut up and skinned, or boneless skinless chicken breasts

Heat the oil in a large nonstick skillet and add the onion. Cook until softened, stirring frequently. Stir in the ketchup, water, brown sugar, Worcestershire sauce, vinegar, chili powder and celery seeds. Bring to a boil and add the chicken, spooning the sauce over the chicken pieces.

Simmer, covered, for 30 minutes for bone-in chicken, or 15 minutes for boneless chicken. Turn the chicken and cook, uncovered, for 15 minutes longer or until cooked through, spooning the sauce over the chicken every 5 minutes. *Yield: 4 servings.*

Tangy Baked Chicken

2 pounds chicken pieces (legs, thighs and breasts)
1 cup honey barbecue sauce
1 cup kumquat, orange or apricot preserves
1 envelope onion soup mix

Arrange the chicken in a single layer in a baking dish. Combine the barbecue sauce, preserves and soup mix in a bowl and pour the barbecue sauce mixture over the chicken. Bake, covered, in a preheated 350-degree oven for 40 minutes. Remove the cover and bake for 20 minutes longer or until the chicken is cooked through. Garnish with whole or sliced kumquats, if desired. *Yield: 6 servings.*

Chinese Chicken with Peppers and Onions

3 whole chicken breasts, split and skinned
3 green or red bell peppers
2 onions
1/4 cup peanut oil
4 (nickel-size) pieces fresh ginger
3 small hot red chiles, or 1/8 teaspoon cayenne pepper
1/4 cup sherry
2 tablespoons soy sauce
1 teaspoon hot sesame oil

Cut the chicken into 1/2-inch pieces. Cut the bell peppers into 1-inch chunks. Slice the onions into quarters and thinly slice the onion quarters.

Heat 2 tablespoons of the peanut oil in a wok or large frying pan until it begins to smoke. Add the ginger, red chiles and chicken and stir-fry for 3 minutes or until the chicken is cooked through. Remove the chicken mixture to a bowl, reserving the pan drippings.

Heat the remaining 2 tablespoons peanut oil with the reserved pan drippings until hot. Add the bell peppers and onion to the hot oil mixture and stir-fry until the onions become slightly translucent. Return the chicken mixture to the wok and stir in the sherry and soy sauce. Stir-fry for 1 minute and sprinkle with the sesame oil. Serve with hot cooked rice. *Yield: 6 servings.*

Chicken Potpie

3 cups (bite-size) pieces cooked chicken
3 hard-cooked eggs, chopped
1 (16-ounce) package frozen peas, thawed
2 cups cooked sliced carrots
2 cups chicken broth
1 (10-ounce) can cream of chicken soup
1 1/2 cups self-rising flour
1 1/2 cups milk
6 tablespoons margarine, melted

Spread the chicken in a 9×13-inch baking dish sprayed with nonstick cooking spray. Top with the eggs, peas and carrots. Mix the broth and soup in a bowl and pour the soup mixture over the layers, mixing to combine.

Whisk the self-rising flour, milk and margarine in a bowl until blended and pour over the top; do not mix. Bake in a preheated 350-degree oven for 45 minutes or until the crust begins to brown. *Yield: 6 servings.*

Italian Chicken

4 fully ripened fresh Florida tomatoes, quartered
1 (8-ounce) can mushrooms, drained
8 (4-ounce) chicken breast fillets
1 envelope onion soup mix
1 (8-ounce) bottle Italian salad dressing
2 bay leaves
1/2 teaspoon oregano

Arrange the tomatoes over the bottom of a 9×13-inch baking dish. Layer with the mushrooms and chicken. Mix the soup mix, salad dressing, bay leaves and oregano in a bowl and pour the salad dressing mixture over the chicken and vegetables. Bake in a preheated 350-degree oven for 1 to 1 1/4 hours or until the chicken is cooked through. Discard the bay leaves before serving. *Yield: 8 servings.*

Chicken and Sausage Casserole

2 pounds chicken pieces
1 (6-ounce) package long grain and wild rice with herbs
1 pound mild bulk pork sausage
1 (10-ounce) can cream of mushroom soup
1 cup canned chicken broth
1 teaspoon salt
1 teaspoon pepper
1 (8-ounce) package herb-seasoned stuffing mix
1/2 cup (1 stick) margarine, melted

Combine the chicken with enough water to cover in a 6- to 8-quart stockpot. Cook, covered, over medium heat, until the juices from the chicken run clear; drain. Cool slightly and chop the chicken into 1/2-inch pieces, discarding the skin and bones. Arrange the chicken in a shallow 2-quart baking dish. Prepare the rice using the package directions.

Brown the sausage in a 10-inch skillet, stirring until crumbly; drain. Stir in the rice, soup, broth, salt and pepper. Spoon the sausage mixture over the chicken and sprinkle with the stuffing mix. Drizzle with the margarine and bake, covered, in a preheated 350-degree oven for 25 minutes. *Yield: 8 servings.*

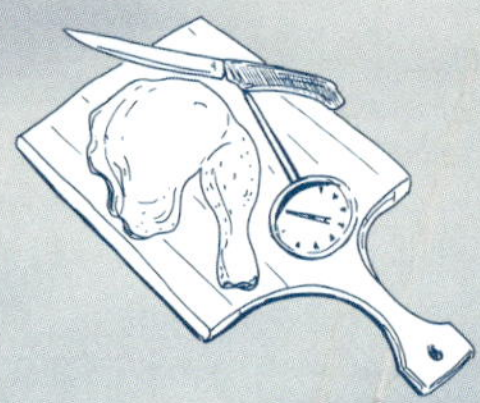

SINGLE MINIMUM INTERNAL TEMPERATURE FOR COOKED POULTRY

The Food Safety and Inspection Service advises that cooking raw poultry to a minimum internal temperature of 165 degrees will eliminate pathogens and viruses. Scientific research indicates that foodborne pathogens and viruses, such as salmonella, Campylobacter, and the avian influenza virus are destroyed when poultry is cooked to this internal temperature. Consumers may certainly cook poultry to higher internal temperatures to meet personal preferences.

Chicken with Spanish-Style Rice and Tomatoes

- 1 tablespoon olive oil
- 1 pound boneless skinless chicken breasts, cut into 1-inch pieces
- 1/4 teaspoon ground pepper
- 2 teaspoons minced garlic
- 1 (8-ounce) package Spanish-style yellow rice
- 2 cups water
- 1 pound fully ripened fresh Florida tomatoes, coarsely chopped (about 2 cups)
- 1 green bell pepper, coarsely chopped
- 1 (15-ounce) can black beans, drained and rinsed
- 1 to 3 teaspoons chopped pickled jalapeño chiles

Heat the olive oil in a large skillet over medium heat. Add the chicken to the hot oil and sprinkle with the pepper. Cook for 5 minutes or until the chicken is almost cooked through, stirring constantly. Add the garlic 2 minutes before the end of the cooking process. Remove the chicken to a platter, reserving the pan drippings.

Stir the rice with seasonings and water into the reserved pan drippings and bring to a boil. Reduce the heat to low and simmer, covered, for 12 minutes or until the water is almost absorbed. Stir in the tomatoes, bell pepper, beans and jalapeño chiles. Top with the chicken and simmer, covered, for 5 minutes longer or until the rice is tender. *Yield: 4 servings.*

Mexican Chicken and Rice

- 1 tablespoon vegetable oil
- 1 pound boneless skinless chicken breasts, chopped
- 1 onion, chopped
- 1 small green bell pepper, chopped
- 1 (10-ounce) package frozen corn, thawed
- 1 cup chicken broth
- 1 cup mild salsa
- 1/4 teaspoon chili powder
- 1 1/2 cups instant rice
- 1/2 cup (2 ounces) shredded Cheddar cheese

Heat the oil in a large skillet over medium-high heat and add the chicken, onion and bell pepper. Cook until the chicken is cooked through, stirring constantly. Add the corn, broth, salsa and chili powder and bring to a boil. Stir in the rice and remove from the heat.

Let stand, covered, for 5 minutes. Fluff with a fork and sprinkle with the cheese. Let stand, covered, for 2 minutes longer or until the cheese melts. *Yield: 6 servings.*

Hot Chicken Salad

- 4 cups chopped cooked chicken breast
- 1 cup chopped celery
- 1 (10-ounce) can reduced-fat reduced sodium cream of chicken soup
- 2 cups reduced-fat mayonnaise
- 1 cup slivered almonds
- 1 (8-ounce) can water chestnuts, drained (optional)
- 1 (8-ounce) can mushroom stems and pieces, drained (optional)
- 1 tablespoon lemon juice
- 2 teaspoons salt (optional)
- 1/2 teaspoon pepper
- 2 cups (8 ounces) shredded Cheddar cheese
- 2 (2-ounce) cans French-fried onions

Combine the chicken, celery, soup, mayonnaise, almonds, water chestnuts, mushrooms, lemon juice, salt and pepper in a bowl and mix well. Spoon the chicken mixture into a 9×13-inch baking dish and sprinkle with the cheese and onions. Bake in a preheated 350-degree oven for 45 minutes or until hot and bubbly. *Yield: 16 servings.*

White Chili

1 pound dried navy beans, or 2 (15-ounce) cans navy or Great Northern beans
6 cups water
4 (8-ounce) boneless skinless chicken breasts
1 large onion, chopped
2 tablespoons ground cumin
1 tablespoon ground white pepper
2 teaspoons oregano
2 garlic cloves, minced
1 teaspoon salt (optional)
2 (4-ounce) cans chopped green chiles, or to taste
1 jalapeño chile, seeded and chopped

Sort and rinse the beans. Combine the beans with enough water to cover by 2 inches in an 8-quart Dutch oven. Soak for 8 hours and drain. Return the beans to the Dutch oven. Add 6 cups water, the chicken, onion, cumin, white pepper, oregano, garlic and salt and bring to a boil. Reduce the heat to low.

Simmer until the chicken is cooked through, stirring occasionally. Remove the chicken to a platter using a slotted spoon, reserving the bean mixture. Chop the chicken into bite-size pieces and return the chicken to the Dutch oven. Stir in the green chiles and jalapeño chile. Add 2 to 3 cups of additional water for a thinner consistency, if desired. Simmer, covered, for 1 hour, stirring occasionally. Ladle into chili bowls. *Yield: 10 servings.*

Curried Chicken Salad

2 cups chopped cooked chicken
3/4 cup dried cranberries
1/2 cup thinly sliced celery
1/4 cup chopped pecans
2 tablespoons thinly sliced green onions
3/4 cup mayonnaise or mayonnaise-type salad dressing
2 teaspoons lime juice
1/2 to 3/4 teaspoon curry powder

Combine the chicken, cranberries, celery, pecans and green onions in a bowl and mix well. Mix the mayonnaise, lime juice and curry powder in a bowl and stir the mayonnaise mixture into the chicken mixture. Chill, covered, until serving time. *Yield: 6 servings.*

Turkey Cheddar Wrap with Spiced Yogurt Dip

1/2 cup plain low-fat yogurt
1/4 cup raisins
1/2 teaspoon curry powder
4 whole wheat tortillas
1 cup (4 ounces) shredded Cheddar cheese
6 ounces sliced turkey breast
1 cup fresh baby spinach leaves
1/2 cup shredded carrots

Mix the yogurt, raisins and curry powder in a bowl. Spread 2 tablespoons of the yogurt mixture to within 1/2 inch of the edge of each tortilla. Layer each tortilla with 1/4 cup of the cheese, 1/4 of the turkey, 1/4 cup of the spinach and 2 tablespoons of the carrots. Roll tightly to enclose the filling. Slice horizontally into bite-size pinwheels or slice diagonally into halves. *Yield: 4 servings.*

Quick Turkey à la King

2 tablespoons butter or margarine
1/2 cup chopped onion
1 (10-ounce) can cream of mushroom soup
8 ounces cream cheese, softened
1/8 teaspoon pepper
1 pound boned cooked turkey, chopped
1 (3-ounce) can sliced mushrooms
1/4 cup chopped green bell pepper
2 tablespoons chopped pimento
2 tablespoons dry sherry
4 hot baked biscuits

Melt the butter in a saucepan and add the onion. Cook until the onion is tender but not brown, stirring frequently. Stir in the soup, cream cheese and pepper. Add the turkey and undrained mushrooms and mix well.

Bring to a boil and stir in the bell pepper, pimento and sherry. Cook until heated through, stirring occasionally. Spoon equal amounts of the turkey mixture over the hot biscuits on each of four serving plates. *Yield: 4 servings.*

HARD-COOKED EGGS NOT HARD-BOILED EGGS

Eggs should never be boiled. They should be cooked gently at no more than a low simmer. Higher heat overcooks the proteins, leaving the egg white tough and rubbery.

Place the eggs in a single layer in a saucepan large enough to prevent overcrowding. Add enough cold water to cover the eggs by at least one inch. Cover the saucepan and quickly bring to boil. Turn off the heat. Remove from the burner, if needed, to prevent further boiling. Let stand, covered with the hot water, for about twelve minutes for medium eggs, fifteen minutes for large eggs, or eighteen minutes for extra-large eggs. Pour off the water, rinse with cold water, and dry before chilling for later use.

If using immediately, drain the eggs and place in a bowl of ice water. Let stand for two minutes. Crack, peel, and enjoy.

Wheat Germ Deviled Eggs

6 hard-cooked eggs
3 tablespoons plain wheat germ
1 tablespoon minced fresh parsley
1/2 cup light mayonnaise
1/2 teaspoon prepared mustard
1/8 teaspoon salt
1/8 teaspoon pepper

Cut the eggs lengthwise into halves. Remove the yolks to a bowl, reserving the egg whites. Mash the egg yolks and stir in the remaining ingredients. Mound the yolk mixture in the egg white halves and arrange on a platter. Chill, covered, until serving time. *Yield: 6 servings.*

Kumquat Gator

1 tablespoon vegetable oil
1 pound cleaned alligator meat, cut into 1/2-inch pieces
Salt and pepper to taste
1 tablespoon vegetable oil
1 tablespoon minced fresh ginger
2 tablespoons minced garlic
15 kumquats, cut into 1/8-inch slices
1/2 cup rice vinegar
1/4 cup soy sauce
2 tablespoons sugar
2 cups fresh green beans, blanched

Heat a large sauté pan over high heat and coat with 1 tablespoon oil. Season the alligator meat with salt and pepper and add to the hot pan. Brown the alligator meat for 2 to 3 minutes and remove to paper towels to drain. Wipe the sauté pan with paper towels and coat with 1 tablespoon oil. Add the ginger and garlic to the sauté pan and sauté for 2 minutes. Stir in the kumquats. Mix the vinegar, soy sauce and sugar in a bowl until the sugar dissolves. Deglaze the sauté pan with the vinegar mixture. Cook until the liquid is reduced by half. Return the alligator meat to the sauté pan. Stir in the green beans and season to taste with salt and pepper. Cook just until heated through. *Yield: 6 servings.*

A Taste of the Seas

A Taste of the Seas

Marinated Amberjack

4 pounds fresh or frozen amberjack fillets or other fish fillets
1/2 cup olive oil or vegetable oil
3 tablespoons lemon juice
2 teaspoons Dijon mustard with white wine
2 garlic cloves, finely chopped
1/2 teaspoon white pepper

Thaw the fillets in the refrigerator if frozen and arrange in a shallow dish. Combine the olive oil, lemon juice, Dijon mustard, garlic and white pepper in a jar with a tight-fitting lid and seal tightly. Shake to mix. Pour the olive oil mixture over the fillets, turning to coat.

Marinate, covered, in the refrigerator for 1 hour, turning once. Remove the fillets from the marinade and arrange in a single layer on a baking sheet, reserving the marinade. Broil 5 to 6 inches from the heat source for 10 minutes or until the fillets flake easily when tested with a fork, basting occasionally during the cooking process with the reserved marinade. *Yield: 8 servings.*

Easy Flounder Fillets

3 pounds fresh or frozen flounder fillets or other fish fillets, skinned
2 tablespoons grated onion
1 1/2 teaspoons salt
1/2 teaspoon pepper
2 large tomatoes, finely chopped
1/4 cup (1/2 stick) butter or margarine, melted
1 cup (4 ounces) shredded Swiss cheese or provolone cheese

Thaw the fillets in the refrigerator if frozen. Arrange the fillets in a single layer on a greased 6×10-inch ovenproof platter. Sprinkle the fillets with the onion, salt and pepper. Top with the tomatoes and drizzle with the butter.

Broil approximately 4 inches from the heat source for 10 to 12 minutes or until the fillets flake easily when tested with a fork. Sprinkle with the cheese and broil for 2 to 3 minutes longer or until the cheese melts. *Yield: 6 servings.*

KUMQUAT GROUPER WITH KUMQUAT POLENTA

Kumquat Polenta
6 cups water
2 teaspoons salt
$1^1/_2$ cups cornmeal
$^1/_2$ cup kumquat purée
2 tablespoons butter

Kumquat Grouper
2 large green cabbage leaves
1 (24-ounce) grouper fillet
$^1/_2$ cup sliced kumquats
1 sprig of basil
1 sprig of oregano
1 tablespoon olive oil

To prepare the polenta, bring the water to a boil in a saucepan and add the salt. Gradually add the cornmeal to the boiling water, whisking constantly. Cook until thickened and tender, stirring frequently. Stir in the purée and butter. Spread the polenta in a 9×9-inch dish and cool for 2 hours. Cut the polenta into 3-inch rounds. Brown the polenta rounds on both sides on a preheated griddle sprayed with nonstick cooking spray, or arrange the rounds on a sheet of foil on the grill rack to warm.

To prepare the grouper, blanch the cabbage leaves in boiling water in a saucepan until bright green. Rinse immediately with cold water to stop the cooking process and pat dry with paper towels. Arrange the fillet skin side down on a work surface. Make 1-inch slits in the fillet and place the sliced kumquats in the slits. Top with the sprigs of basil and oregano and drizzle with the olive oil.

Lay the fillet on one cabbage leaf and cover with the remaining cabbage leaf. Secure the cabbage with kitchen string. Grill for 8 minutes per side. Remove the fillet to a plate and open just before serving. Serve with the polenta rounds.
Yield: 6 servings.

Grouper Parmesan

- 2 pounds fresh or frozen grouper fillets or other fish fillets
- 1 cup low-fat sour cream
- 1/4 cup (1 ounce) grated Parmesan cheese
- 1 tablespoon lemon juice
- 1 tablespoon grated onion
- 1/2 teaspoon salt
- 1/8 teaspoon hot red pepper sauce

Thaw the fillets in the refrigerator if frozen. Remove the skin and cut the fillets into six equal portions. Arrange the fillets in a single layer in a greased 8×12-inch baking dish. Combine the sour cream, cheese, lemon juice, onion, salt and hot sauce in a bowl and spread over the fillets.

Bake in a preheated 350-degree oven for 25 to 30 minutes or until the fillets flake easily when tested with a fork. Garnish with chopped fresh parsley and paprika. *Yield: 6 servings.*

Festive Mullet

- 2 pounds fresh or frozen mullet fillets
- 1 cup French or Russian salad dressing
- 1 1/2 cups crushed cheese crackers or nacho-flavored tortilla chips
- 2 tablespoons vegetable oil
- Paprika to taste

Thaw the fillets in the refrigerator if frozen. Remove the skin and cut the fillets into six equal portions. Dip the fillets in the salad dressing and coat with the cracker crumbs. Arrange in a single layer on a greased 12×15-inch baking sheet. Drizzle with the oil and sprinkle with paprika.

Bake in a preheated 500-degree oven for 10 to 12 minutes or until the fillets flake easily when tested with a fork. Garnish with lemon or lime wedges that have been coated with chopped fresh parsley. *Yield: 6 servings.*

Smoky Salmon Cheese Ball

2 (6-ounce) cans pink salmon, drained
8 ounces cream cheese, softened
2 tablespoons minced onion
1 tablespoon parsley flakes
1 tablespoon lemon juice
3/4 teaspoon celery salt
1/2 teaspoon liquid smoke
1/2 teaspoon garlic powder
1/2 cup pecans, finely chopped
2 tablespoons minced fresh parsley

Discard the bones and skin from the salmon. Combine the salmon, cream cheese, onion, parsley flakes, lemon juice, celery salt, liquid smoke and garlic powder in a bowl and mix well. Chill, covered, for 1 hour or longer.

Shape the salmon mixture into a ball and coat with the pecans and the parsley. Serve with assorted party crackers. *Yield: 12 (1-ounce) servings.*

Fish Chowder

1 1/2 pounds fresh or frozen grouper
1 cup water
2 (10-ounce) cans cream of potato soup
1 quart low-fat milk
1 (14- to 16-ounce) can whole kernel corn
1 or 2 small jalapeño chiles, seeded and chopped
2 tablespoons margarine
1 tablespoon dried minced onion
1 small bay leaf
1/2 teaspoon salt
1/8 teaspoon pepper

Thaw the grouper in the refrigerator if frozen. Discard the skin and cut into 1-inch pieces. Bring the water to a boil in a 2-quart saucepan and add the grouper. Simmer for 8 to 10 minutes or until the grouper flakes easily when tested with a fork.

Add the soup, milk, undrained corn, jalapeño chiles, margarine, onion, bay leaf, salt and pepper to the grouper mixture and cook just until heated through, stirring occasionally. Discard the bay leaf and ladle the soup into bowls. Garnish with paprika. You may substitute pompano or bass fillets for the grouper. *Yield: 6 servings.*

JAMBALAYA

1 pound smoked beef sausage
3 large onions, chopped
1 1/2 cups chopped green bell pepper
1 cup chopped celery
2 garlic cloves, minced
1 1/2 cups canned diced tomatoes with juice
1 cup long grain rice (do not use instant)
3 tablespoons tomato paste
1 bay leaf
1 tablespoon chopped fresh parsley
1 teaspoon thyme
1 teaspoon salt
1/4 teaspoon cayenne pepper
1 1/2 cups water
1 1/2 pounds shrimp, peeled and deveined

Brown the sausage with the onions in a stockpot, stirring until the sausage is crumbly and the onions are tender. Stir in the bell pepper, celery and garlic. Sauté until the vegetables are tender. Add the tomatoes, rice, tomato paste, bay leaf, parsley, thyme, salt and cayenne pepper; mix well.

Stir the water into the sausage mixture and bring to a boil. Add the shrimp and reduce the heat to low. Cook for 30 to 45 minutes or until the rice is tender, stirring occasionally. Discard the bay leaf. Ladle into soup bowls. *Yield: 8 servings.*

SEAFOOD CHOWDER (BOUILLABAISSE)

1 onion, chopped
2 slices bacon, chopped
4 cups water
1 (16-ounce) package frozen stew vegetables
2 pounds deveined peeled shrimp
1 (12-ounce) can evaporated milk
2 tablespoons butter
Salt and pepper to taste

Cook the onion and bacon in a stockpot until brown, stirring frequently. Add the water and bring to a boil. Stir in the vegetables and return to a boil.

Boil for 10 minutes. Add the shrimp and cook for 5 minutes longer or until the shrimp turn pink. Stir in the evaporated milk and butter and cook just until the butter melts. Remove from the heat and season to taste with salt and pepper. Ladle into soup bowls. You may substitute scallops or clams for the shrimp. *Yield: 6 servings.*

Baked Fish Guamanian Style

2 tablespoons vegetable oil
1 1/2 pounds tuna, salmon or any variety fish fillets
1/2 cup ketchup
1/2 cup orange juice
2 tablespoons lemon juice
2 tablespoons finely chopped celery
2 tablespoons finely chopped onion
1 garlic clove, minced

Heat the oil in a large skillet and add the fillets. Cook until light brown on both sides. Arrange the fillets in a single layer in a 9×13-inch baking dish.

Combine the ketchup, orange juice, lemon juice, celery, onion and garlic in a bowl and mix well. Pour over the fillets and bake in a preheated 350-degree oven for 45 minutes or until the fillets flake easily when tested with a fork. *Yield: 10 servings.*

Crabby Potatoes

4 baking potatoes
1/2 cup milk
1/3 cup butter or margarine, softened
1 teaspoon salt
1/8 teaspoon cayenne pepper
1 cup (4 ounces) shredded Cheddar cheese
1 (6-ounce) can crab meat, drained and flaked
4 teaspoons grated onion
1/2 teaspoon paprika

Bake the potatoes in the oven or microwave until tender. Cool slightly and cut the potatoes lengthwise into halves. Scoop out the pulp carefully, leaving the shells intact and reserving the pulp.

Combine the reserved pulp, milk, butter, salt and cayenne pepper in a mixing bowl and beat until blended. Fold in the cheese, crab meat and onion. Spoon the crab meat mixture into the reserved shells and sprinkle with the paprika. Arrange the stuffed potatoes in a 9×12-inch baking dish and bake in a preheated 400-degree oven for 15 minutes or until light brown. *Yield: 8 servings.*

Hot Crab, Red Pepper and Onion Dip

- 1 cup (4 ounces) shredded mozzarella cheese
- 8 ounces cream cheese, softened
- 1 teaspoon garlic powder
- 1 teaspoon Italian seasoning
- 1 red bell pepper, chopped
- 1 small onion, finely chopped
- 1 (6-ounce) can crab meat, drained, shells and cartilage removed
- 1 cup chopped fresh parsley (optional)
- 1/2 cup (2 ounces) shredded mozzarella cheese
- 1 package small low-fat wheat crackers

Combine 1 cup mozzarella cheese, the cream cheese, garlic powder and Italian seasoning in a bowl and mix well. Gently stir in the bell pepper, onion, crab meat and 1 cup parsley. Spread in a 9-inch round baking dish.

Bake in a preheated 375-degree oven for 20 minutes or until heated through and light brown on top. Remove from the oven and sprinkle with 1/2 cup mozzarella cheese. Garnish with additional chopped fresh parsley and serve with the wheat crackers. *Yield: 24 (2 tablespoons dip and 8 crackers).*

HERB SHAKER FOR FISH

*For **Herbed Celery Mix**, combine 1/4 cup dried minced onion, 1 tablespoon dill seeds, 1 1/2 teaspoons celery seeds and 1/4 teaspoon tarragon in a blender. Process for one minute at high speed or until of a powdery consistency. Store in a shaker. You may also use on meat, poultry, and vegetables.*

Crab Casserole

8 slices dry or toasted bread, cubed
2 (7-ounce) cans crab meat, drained and flaked
1 cup chopped celery
1 green bell pepper, finely chopped
1 onion, finely chopped
1/2 cup mayonnaise
1/2 teaspoon salt
4 eggs, lightly beaten
3 cups milk
1 (10-ounce) can cream of mushroom soup
1/2 cup (2 ounces) shredded Cheddar cheese

Arrange half of the bread cubes in a 9×13-inch baking dish sprayed with nonstick cooking spray or coated with butter. Combine the crab meat, celery, bell pepper, onion, mayonnaise and salt in a bowl and mix well. Spread over the prepared layer and top with the remaining bread cubes.

Whisk the eggs, milk and soup in a bowl just until blended and pour over the prepared layers. Chill, covered with foil, for 2 to 10 hours. Bake, covered, in a preheated 325-degree oven for 1 1/4 hours. Remove the foil and sprinkle with the cheese. Bake for 10 minutes longer or until brown. *Yield: 8 servings.*

NOTE: You may add 1/2 cup slivered almonds to the crab meat mixture.

Crab and Tomato Quesadillas

1 1/2 cups (6 ounces) shredded Monterey Jack cheese
2 ounces low-fat cream cheese, softened
1/2 cup chopped fresh cilantro
2 tablespoons orange juice
1 teaspoon grated orange zest
1 teaspoon grated lemon zest
Salt and pepper to taste
8 ounces crab meat, drained and flaked
1 cup chopped seeded fully ripened fresh
 Florida plum tomatoes
1/2 cup chopped green onions
1 tablespoon minced seeded jalapeño chile
8 (7- or 8-inch) flour tortillas

Combine the Monterey Jack cheese, cream cheese, cilantro, orange juice, orange zest and lemon zest in a bowl and mix well. Season with salt and pepper. Chill, covered, for up to 1 day. Let stand until room temperature. Gently mix the crab meat, tomatoes, green onions and jalapeño chile in a large bowl.

Spread the cheese mixture evenly on one side of each tortilla. Spread the crab meat mixture evenly over the cheese mixture and season to taste with salt and pepper. Fold the tortilla in half and press gently to seal. Arrange the quesadillas on a baking sheet and bake in a preheated 350-degree oven for 7 minutes or until heated through, turning halfway through the baking process if needed to prevent overbrowning.
Yield: 4 (2-quesadilla) servings.

LIMITING *TRANS* FATS

Decreasing heart disease risk is a primary goal of many Extension nutrition programs. High levels of low-density lipoprotein cholesterol (LDL) in the blood contributes to the risk for heart disease. Diet affects LDL levels, so what we eat is important.

Trans fats increase LDL and their intake should be limited. Trans fats are formed when liquid oils are partially hydrogenated to form solid fats, like margarine. The major sources of trans fat in the American diet are foods made with partially hydrogenated oils–cakes, cookies, crackers, pies, and breads. Beginning in January 2006, trans fat is required to be listed on the Nutrition Facts panel on food labels. Many food manufacturers have been reformulating their products to reduce trans fat content.

Crab Quiche

- 8 ounces crab meat, drained and flaked
- 1/2 cup evaporated milk
- 1/2 cup mayonnaise-type salad dressing or mayonnaise
- 2 eggs, lightly beaten
- 1/2 cup chopped green onions
- 1/2 cup chopped green bell pepper
- 1 1/2 cups (6 ounces) shredded Cheddar cheese, Swiss cheese or Monterey Jack cheese
- 1 unbaked (9-inch) pie shell

Combine the crab meat, evaporated milk, salad dressing, eggs, green onions, bell pepper and cheese in a bowl in the order listed and mix well. Spoon the crab meat mixture into the pie shell and bake in a preheated 350-degree oven for 40 minutes. Serve immediately or freeze for future use. You may double the recipe for two quiches. *Yield: 8 servings.*

Crab Meat Quiche

- 1 pound blue crab meat, drained and flaked
- 1 cup (4 ounces) shredded Swiss cheese or provolone cheese
- 1/3 cup finely chopped green onions
- 1 tablespoon chopped fresh parsley
- 1 tablespoon finely chopped celery
- 3/4 teaspoon salt
- 1/2 teaspoon Worcestershire sauce
- 1/2 teaspoon dry mustard
- 1/4 teaspoon freshly ground black pepper
- 1/8 teaspoon cayenne pepper
- 2 cups half-and-half
- 4 eggs, beaten
- 2 unbaked (9-inch) pie shells

Combine the crab meat, cheese, green onions, parsley, celery, salt, Worcestershire sauce, dry mustard, black pepper and cayenne pepper in a bowl and mix well. Stir in the half-and-half and eggs.

Pour the crab meat mixture evenly into the pie shells. Bake in a preheated 450-degree oven for 7 to 10 minutes. Reduce the oven temperature to 350 degrees and bake for 20 minutes longer. *Yield: 16 servings.*

Delectable Oyster Stew

2 pints fresh or frozen oysters
2 slices turkey bacon
1 tablespoon olive oil
1/3 cup chopped onion
1 (10-ounce) can reduced-fat cream of potato soup
3 cups light cream or half-and-half
1 1/4 teaspoons salt
1/8 teaspoon white pepper

Thaw the oysters in the refrigerator if frozen. Drain, reserving the liquor. Fry the bacon in a skillet until brown and crisp; drain. Break the slices crosswise into thirds. Heat the olive oil in a saucepan and add the onion. Cook until tender and stir in the reserved oyster liquor, soup, cream, salt and white pepper.

Simmer until heated through, stirring occasionally. Add the oysters and bacon and simmer for 5 minutes longer or until the edges of the oysters begin to curl. Ladle into soup bowls and garnish with chopped fresh parsley. *Yield: 6 servings.*

Baked Scallops with Tomatoes

1 pound fresh or frozen scallops
3 fully ripened fresh Florida tomatoes, each cut crosswise into 4 slices
1 teaspoon salt
1/8 teaspoon pepper
2 teaspoons celery salt
2 teaspoons Worcestershire sauce
2 tablespoons margarine or butter, melted
3/4 cup (3 ounces) shredded Cheddar cheese or mozzarella cheese

Thaw the scallops in the refrigerator if frozen. Discard any shell pieces. Cut the large scallops into halves and place in a bowl.

Arrange the tomato slices over the bottom of a greased 7×11-inch baking pan and sprinkle with the salt and pepper. Mix the celery salt, Worcestershire sauce and margarine in a bowl and pour over the scallops, turning to coat.

Spoon the scallop mixture over the tomatoes and sprinkle with the cheese. Bake in a preheated-450 degree oven for 15 to 20 minutes or until the scallops are tender and the cheese is brown. *Yield: 6 servings.*

Shrimp Casserole

- $^1/_3$ cup butter
- $1^1/_2$ cups chopped green onions
- 1 cup chopped celery
- 1 tablespoon minced garlic
- 3 cups cooked rice
- 1 (10-ounce) can cream of mushroom soup
- 2 slices bread, slightly moistened and torn into pieces
- $^1/_2$ cup water
- 3 tablespoons chopped fresh parsley
- 1 (12-ounce) package frozen shrimp, thawed
- 1 teaspoon salt
- $^1/_4$ teaspoon pepper
- $^3/_4$ cup bread crumbs
- 3 tablespoons butter, melted

Melt $^1/_3$ cup butter in a deep skillet and add the green onions, celery and garlic. Cook until the onion is tender, stirring frequently. Stir in the rice, soup, bread, water and parsley. Cook over medium heat for 10 minutes, stirring occasionally. Stir in the shrimp, salt and pepper and spoon into a $1^1/_2$-quart baking dish. Toss the bread crumbs and 3 tablespoons butter in a bowl until coated. Sprinkle the bread crumbs over the prepared layer and bake in a preheated 375-degree oven for 30 minutes. *Yield: 6 servings.*

Shrimp Pilaf

- 1 (20-ounce) can tomatoes
- $^1/_2$ cup chopped onion
- $^1/_2$ cup chopped celery
- 2 tablespoons ketchup
- 2 tablespoons Worcestershire sauce
- 2 tablespoons butter or margarine
- 2 teaspoons lemon juice
- 2 teaspoons salt
- 1 cup rice
- 1 pound shrimp, peeled and deveined

Combine the undrained tomatoes, onion and celery in a large saucepan and bring to a boil. Reduce the heat to low and simmer, covered, for 15 minutes, stirring occasionally. Stir in the ketchup, Worcestershire sauce, butter, lemon juice and salt.

Bring to a boil and stir in the rice. Reduce the heat to low and simmer for 15 minutes, stirring occasionally. Stir in the shrimp and cook for 15 minutes or until the liquid is absorbed. *Yield: 4 servings.*

Shrimp Macaroni Salad

12 ounces fresh or frozen deveined peeled cooked shrimp
2 cups cooked shell macaroni
1 cup chopped cauliflower
1 cup sliced celery
1/4 cup chopped fresh parsley
1/4 cup sweet pickle relish
1/2 cup reduced-fat mayonnaise or salad dressing
3 tablespoons garlic French salad dressing
1 tablespoon lemon juice
1/4 cup chopped red onion
1 teaspoon celery seeds
1 teaspoon salt
1/4 teaspoon pepper

Cut the shrimp into bite-size pieces if needed. Combine the shrimp, pasta, cauliflower, celery, parsley and pickle relish in a bowl and mix well. Mix the mayonnaise, salad dressing and lemon juice in a bowl. Stir in the onion, celery seeds, salt and pepper.

Add the mayonnaise mixture to the shrimp mixture and toss gently to combine. Chill, covered, until serving time. Serve on a bed of mixed salad greens garnished with hard-cooked sliced egg. *Yield: 6 servings.*

Shrimp and Spinach Pita Pizzas

1/2 teaspoon olive oil
1/4 cup thinly sliced red onion
3 cups chopped fresh spinach
1/4 teaspoon oregano
2 (6-inch) pita rounds
1 1/2 cups (6 ounces) shredded light mozzarella cheese
2 fully ripened fresh Florida plum tomatoes, sliced
10 large shrimp, cooked, peeled and deveined

Heat the olive oil in a small skillet over medium heat. Add the onion to the hot oil and cook for 1 minute. Stir in the spinach and oregano and cook for 1 minute longer or until the spinach wilts. Remove from the heat. Sprinkle each pita round with 1/4 cup of the cheese. Layer each round with equal amounts of the spinach mixture, tomatoes, shrimp and remaining 1 cup cheese. Arrange the pizzas on a baking sheet and bake in a preheated 400-degree oven for 10 minutes or until the cheese melts. This recipe is a good source of calcium. *Yield: 2 servings.*

Shrimply Delicious Quiche

12 ounces fresh or frozen deveined peeled rock or bay shrimp
2 cups water
1 tablespoon salt
1 1/2 cups sliced fresh mushrooms
2/3 cup sliced green onions
1 tablespoon olive oil
1 1/2 cups half-and-half
1/4 cup (1/2 stick) butter or margarine, melted
4 eggs
1 teaspoon salt
1/8 teaspoon dry mustard
1 cup (4 ounces) shredded mozzarella cheese
2 unbaked (9-inch) pie shells

Thaw the shrimp in the refrigerator if frozen. Bring the water and 1 tablespoon salt to a boil in a large saucepan. Add the shrimp and cook for 30 seconds; drain. Rinse with cold water for 1 to 2 minutes and drain. Finely chop the shrimp with a knife or chop in a food processor. Sauté the mushrooms and green onions in the olive oil in a skillet until tender. Combine the half-and-half, butter, eggs, 1 teaspoon salt and the dry mustard in a mixing bowl and beat until blended.

Layer half of the shrimp, half of the mushroom mixture and half of the cheese in each of the pie shells. Pour half of the egg mixture in each pie shell and bake in a preheated 425-degree oven for 15 minutes. Reduce the oven temperature to 300 degrees and bake for 30 minutes longer. Let stand for 15 minutes before serving. *Yield: 16 servings.*

Creamy Seafood Medley

2 tablespoons butter or margarine
8 ounces shrimp, peeled and deveined
8 ounces fresh bay scallops
1/4 cup chopped onion
1 (10-ounce) can cream of shrimp soup
1/4 cup light cream
3 tablespoons buttered bread crumbs

Melt the butter in a skillet and add the shrimp, scallops and onion. Sauté until the shrimp and scallops are opaque and the onion is tender. Stir in the soup and cream and cook for several minutes, stirring occasionally. Spoon into four ramekins and sprinkle with the bread crumbs. Broil until brown on top. You may sprinkle with 3 tablespoons shredded Cheddar cheese instead of the bread crumbs. *Yield: 4 servings.*

Delicious Dairy Dishes

Delicious Dairy Dishes

Baked Spinach and Artichoke Dip

- 1 (10-ounce) package frozen chopped spinach, thawed and drained
- 1 (14-ounce) can artichoke hearts, drained and chopped
- 1 cup plain low-fat yogurt
- 1 cup (4 ounces) shredded part-skim mozzarella cheese
- 1/4 cup chopped green onions
- 1 garlic clove, minced
- 2 tablespoons chopped red bell pepper

Press the excess moisture from the spinach. Combine the spinach, artichokes, yogurt, cheese, green onions and garlic in a bowl and mix well. Spoon the spinach mixture into a 1-quart baking dish or 9-inch baking dish.

Bake in a preheated 350-degree oven for 20 to 25 minutes or until heated through. Sprinkle with the bell pepper and serve with toasted party bread and/or whole grain crackers. *Yield: 8 servings.*

Cheese Ring with Strawberry Preserves

- 16 ounces medium Cheddar cheese, shredded
- 1 cup chopped pecans
- 1 onion, chopped
- 3/4 cup mayonnaise
- 1/2 teaspoon hot red pepper sauce
- 1/2 teaspoon garlic juice
- 1 cup strawberry preserves

Mix the cheese, pecans and onion in a bowl. Add the mayonnaise, hot sauce and garlic juice and stir until combined. Shape the cheese mixture into a ring on a serving platter. Chill, covered, until serving time.

Spoon the preserves into a small bowl and place the bowl in the center of the cheese ring. Serve with assorted party crackers. *Yield: 16 servings.*

CHEESE TOAST

Serve as an accompaniment to meals or as an appetizer. Arrange four diagonally cut 1/2-inch-thick-slices French bread or baguette slices on a baking sheet. Mix 2 tablespoons softened butter, 1/2 teaspoon minced garlic and 1/8 teaspoon paprika in a bowl and spread the butter mixture on one side of each of the bread slices. Sprinkle with a mixture of 1/4 cup shredded Swiss cheese and 1 tablespoon grated Parmesan cheese. Bake in a preheated 400-degree oven for 10 to 15 minutes or until the bread is crisp and the cheese is bubbly.

Cheese Lover's Pizza Squares

1 (13-ounce) can refrigerator pizza dough
1 cup ricotta cheese
2 cups (8 ounces) shredded part-skim mozzarella cheese
2 ounces turkey pepperoni
2 fully ripened fresh Florida plum tomatoes, thinly sliced
1 cup sliced yellow bell pepper
1 teaspoon oregano
2 tablespoons chopped fresh parsley

Press the pizza dough into a 10×15-inch baking pan and bake in a preheated 400-degree oven for 12 minutes. Maintain the oven temperature.

Spread the ricotta cheese over the baked layer and top with the mozzarella cheese, pepperoni, tomatoes, bell pepper and oregano. Bake for 6 minutes or until the cheese melts. Sprinkle with the parsley and cut into squares. Serve immediately.
Yield: 10 servings.

Confetti Quesadillas with Cilantro Yogurt Dip

Cilantro Yogurt Dip
2 cups plain nonfat yogurt
1/4 cup finely minced fresh cilantro
1/2 teaspoon salt

Quesadillas
12 soft corn tortillas
1 cup (4 ounces) shredded part-skim Colby cheese
1 cup (4 ounces) shredded part-skim Monterey Jack cheese
1/2 cup fresh corn kernels or black beans, drained
1 red bell pepper, finely minced
1 jalapeño chile, finely minced
1/2 cup coarsely chopped fresh cilantro

To prepare the dip, line a large strainer with a coffee filter or paper towel and place over a bowl. Pour the yogurt into the strainer and let stand at room temperature for 1 hour or until some of the liquid has drained and the yogurt is the consistency of sour cream, discarding the liquid. Spoon the yogurt into a bowl and stir in the cilantro and salt. Makes about 1 1/2 cups.

To prepare the quesadillas, lay six of the tortillas on a work surface. Layer equal amounts of the Colby cheese, Monterey Jack cheese, corn, bell pepper, jalapeño chile and cilantro on each of the tortillas. Cover each with one of the remaining six tortillas.

Cook one quesadilla at a time in a large preheated skillet for 3 minutes or until light golden brown and turn. Cook for 1 minute longer or until the other side is golden brown. Repeat the process with the remaining quesadillas. Cut each quesadilla into wedges and serve with the dip. You may alernatively grill over hot coals, if desired. *Yield: 6 (1-quesadilla and 1/4-cup dip) servings.*

NOTE: Straining yogurt gives you a nonfat version of sour cream with a light tang that blends nicely with the cilantro. Serve with chili and other spicy dishes as well.

Grilled Goat Cheese Sandwiches

4 ounces goat cheese
4 ounces cream cheese
8 slices party bread
1 tablespoon butter, softened

Mix the goat cheese and cream cheese in a bowl until blended. Spread the cheese mixture on one side of each of the bread slices. Stack two bread slices cheese sides facing in to form a sandwich. Repeat the process with the remaining bread slices.

Spread the butter on both sides of the sandwiches. Grill the sandwiches in a sauté pan until the cheese is hot, turning once. Serve with Roasted Strawberry and Tomato Soup on page 128. *Yield: 4 servings.*

Choco-Nana Milk Mixer

2 cups 1% milk
1 (4-ounce) package chocolate instant pudding mix
1 tablespoon creamy peanut butter
1 banana, chopped
1 1/2 cups 1% milk

Combine 2 cups milk, the pudding mix, peanut butter and banana into a container with a tight-fitting lid and shake until combined. Or, process the banana mixture in a blender at medium speed for 1 minute or until smooth.

Pour the banana mixture into a pitcher and stir in 1 1/2 cups milk. Serve immediately or chill, covered, until serving time; stir before serving. Thin with additional milk, if desired, as the mixture will thicken after standing. *Yield: 4 servings.*

Festive Fruity Flavored Milk

1 cup fat-free milk or 1% milk
2 tablespoons apricot, blackberry, raspberry or strawberry fruit syrup

Mix the milk and syrup in a pitcher. Pour into two glasses and serve immediately. *Yield: 2 servings.*

NOTE: Fruit syrups are available in natural and artificially flavored varieties. They are usually located in your local supermarket on the aisle with the pancake mixes. Try experimenting with different brands of fruit syrups until you find the one that provides the perfect color and flavor for your milk.

Double Pineapple Breakfast Shake

3 cups chopped fresh or canned pineapple
$1\frac{1}{2}$ cups lemon yogurt
1 ripe banana, sliced
$\frac{1}{4}$ teaspoon ground cinnamon

Combine the pineapple, yogurt, banana and cinnamon in a blender or food processor. Process until smooth. Pour into two glasses and serve immediately. *Yield: 2 (12-ounce) servings.*

DAIRY PRODUCERS CARE

Dairy farmers are committed to their animals, the environment, and the safety of the milk supply. Dairy cows receive a well-balanced and nutritious diet, plus sound medical care to assure their comfort and well-being. They are provided with clean barns where they live, eat, and sleep. And to provide relief on those hot Florida days, farmers utilize systems of fans and water misters to keep their animals cool.

Producers care greatly about their environment and go to great lengths to assure that they are good stewards of the land. They also take measures to keep America's milk supply among the safest and purest in the world.

For many producers, their dairy farm also serves as their home, and they work diligently to be good community leaders and neighbors. Farmers share a heritage of responsible production and a commitment to preserve their legacy for the future.

MOVING TO LOW-FAT DAIRY

Milk, cheese, and yogurt are nutrient-packed foods. They provide high-quality protein, calcium, and riboflavin, and fortified milk provides vitamins A and D. People who drink milk tend to have higher quality diets overall.

With rising rates of obesity many people want to decrease calorie and fat intake, without sacrificing the nutrient quality of their diets. Low-fat and fat-free milk, yogurt, and cheese provide the nutrients of full-fat dairy foods, without the extra fat and calories. Federal dietary guidelines recommend daily consumption of 3 cups (or equivalent) of low-fat or fat-free milk, yogurt, or cheese for everyone nine years of age and older.

Breakfast Smoothie

1 cup plain nonfat yogurt
1 cup 1% milk or fat-free milk
$1\frac{1}{4}$ cups fresh or frozen whole strawberries
1 peach, peeled and sliced, or $\frac{3}{4}$ cup frozen peach slices
2 teaspoons vanilla extract
2 tablespoons chopped walnuts

Combine the yogurt, milk, strawberries, peach and vanilla in a blender and process for 15 to 20 seconds or until puréed. Pour the smoothie evenly into two tall glasses and top each with 1 tablespoon of the walnuts. Garnish each smoothie with one fresh whole strawberry and serve immediately.
Yield: 2 (10-ounce) servings.

NOTE: For a thicker consistency, substitute 1 sliced small banana for the peach.

Strawberry Yogurt Smoothie

1 1/2 cups fat-free milk, chilled
1 1/2 teaspoons strawberry low-calorie drink mix
1 cup vanilla low-fat yogurt
1 cup frozen strawberries

Place the milk, soft drink mix, yogurt and strawberries in a blender in the order listed. Process at high speed until smooth and pour into four glasses. Serve immediately. *Yield: 4 servings.*

Coffee Punch

2 quarts strong-brewed coffee
2 cups milk
1/2 cup sugar
1 teaspoon vanilla extract
1 cup whipping cream
1 cup dark rum (optional)
1 quart vanilla or chocolate ice cream

Combine the coffee, milk, sugar and vanilla in a bowl and stir until the sugar dissolves. Chill, covered, in the refrigerator.

Just before serving stir the whipping cream and rum into the coffee mixture. Scoop the ice cream into a punch bowl and pour the coffee mixture over the ice cream. Ladle into punch cups. *Yield: 20 (6-ounce) servings.*

MICROWAVE WHITE SAUCE

This is a fail-proof method for a smooth, creamy sauce that can be used on any vegetable. A basic white sauce is also the beginning for a variety of other sauces such as cheese, curry, or horseradish.

Combine 2 tablespoons butter, 2 tablespoons all-purpose flour and 1/2 teaspoon salt in a 1-quart microwave-safe bowl. Microwave on High for 2 minutes, stirring after 1 minute. Gradually stir in 1 cup milk and microwave on High for 3 1/2 to 4 1/2 minutes or until thick and bubbly, stirring at 1 minute intervals.

Farmer's Casserole

3 cups frozen shredded hash brown potatoes, thawed
3/4 cup (3 ounces) shredded reduced-fat Monterey Jack cheese
1 cup chopped cooked ham
1/4 cup chopped green onions
4 eggs, or equivalent amount of egg substitute
1 (12-ounce) can evaporated skim milk
1/4 teaspoon pepper
1/8 teaspoon salt

Spread the potatoes over the bottom of an 8×8-inch baking dish. Sprinkle with the cheese, ham and green onions. Whisk the eggs, evaporated skim milk, pepper and salt in a bowl until blended and pour over the prepared layers.

Chill, covered, for 2 to 10 hours. Let stand at room temperature for 30 minutes. Bake, uncovered, in a preheated 350-degree oven for 55 to 60 minutes or until a knife inserted near the center comes out clean. *Yield: 6 servings.*

Mexican Egg Casserole

10 eggs, or equivalent amount of egg substitute
1/3 cup butter, melted
1/2 cup self-rising flour
1/2 teaspoon baking powder
1/2 teaspoon salt
2 cups low-fat cottage cheese
12 ounces Monterey Jack cheese, shredded
1 (8-ounce) can chopped green chiles, drained

Whisk the eggs in a bowl until blended and stir in the butter. Add a mixture of the self-rising flour, baking powder and salt and mix well. Stir in the cottage cheese, Monterey Jack cheese and green chiles.

Spoon into a greased 9×13-inch baking dish. Bake in a preheated 350-degree oven for 35 minutes or until the center is set. Serve immediately. *Yield: 12 servings.*

Cheddar Spinach Quiche

1 (10-ounce) package frozen spinach, cooked
2 cups (8 ounces) shredded sharp Cheddar cheese
2 tablespoons all-purpose flour
1 cup milk
2 eggs, beaten
3 slices bacon, crisp-cooked and crumbled
1/8 teaspoon cayenne pepper
1 unbaked (9-inch) pie shell

Drain the spinach on paper towels or in a colander. Toss the cheese with the flour in a bowl. Stir the spinach, milk, eggs, bacon and cayenne pepper into the cheese mixture.

Spoon into the pie shell and bake in a preheated 350-degree oven for 1 hour. Garnish with additional bacon, if desired. *Yield: 6 servings.*

BASIC WHITE SAUCE VARIATIONS

*To make a **Cheese Sauce**, stir 1 cup shredded sharp Cheddar cheese and $\frac{1}{8}$ teaspoon cayenne pepper into the finished white sauce. Microwave on High for 1 to 2 minutes or until blended.*

*To make a **Curry Sauce**, mix 2 to 3 teaspoons curry powder with the all-purpose flour and proceed with the basic white sauce recipe.*

*To make a **Horseradish Sauce**, mix 1 to 2 teaspoons cream-style horseradish with the finished white sauce.*

TOMATO QUICHE

2 eggs
2 cups (8 ounces) shredded Swiss cheese or Cheddar cheese
$1\frac{1}{2}$ cups milk
$\frac{1}{2}$ cup chopped onion
$1\frac{1}{4}$ teaspoons salt
$\frac{1}{4}$ teaspoon pepper
1 fully ripened fresh Florida tomato, chopped
1 baked (9-inch) pie shell
1 fully ripened fresh Florida tomato, sliced

Lightly beat the eggs in a bowl. Stir in the cheese, milk, onion, salt and pepper. Add the chopped tomato and mix well. Pour into the pie shell and bake in a preheated 325-degree oven for 30 minutes. Maintain the oven temperature. Arrange the sliced tomato over the baked layer.

Bake for 25 minutes longer or until a knife inserted in the center comes out clean. Let stand for 10 minutes before slicing. *Yield: 4 servings.*

French Toast Casserole

1 loaf French bread, cut into 1/2-inch cubes
8 ounces cream cheese, cubed
8 eggs, or equivalent amount of egg substitute
2 1/2 cups whole milk, fat-free milk, light cream or half-and-half
6 tablespoons butter, melted
1/4 cup maple syrup

Spread half the bread cubes in a greased shallow 3-quart baking dish. Layer with the cream cheese and remaining bread cubes.

Combine the eggs, milk, butter and syrup in a blender and process until blended. Pour the egg mixture over the prepared layers, lightly pressing the bread cubes into the liquid to ensure coverage.

Chill, covered with plastic wrap, for 2 to 24 hours. Bake in a preheated 325-degree oven for 35 to 40 minutes or until the center is set and the edges are golden brown. Serve with additional syrup. *Yield: 8 servings.*

Cheese Garlic Biscuits

2 cups baking mix
2/3 cup milk
1/2 cup (2 ounces) shredded Cheddar cheese
1/2 teaspoon garlic powder
1/4 cup (1/2 stick) butter, melted

Combine the baking mix, milk, cheese and 1/4 teaspoon of the garlic powder in a bowl and mix until a soft dough forms. Beat for 30 seconds. Drop by rounded spoonfuls onto an ungreased baking sheet.

Bake in a preheated 450-degree oven for 8 to 10 minutes or until golden brown. Mix the remaining 1/4 teaspoon garlic powder and butter in a bowl and brush the butter mixture over the warm biscuits. Serve immediately. *Yield: 10 biscuits.*

Baked Pears with Vanilla Yogurt and Granola

3 (6-ounce) containers vanilla low-fat yogurt
2 pears (Bartlett or Anjou)
1 cup water
1/2 cup apple juice
1 tablespoon honey
1/2 cup low-fat granola

Line a colander with paper towels and place over a bowl. Spoon the yogurt into the colander and drain for 30 to 60 minutes. Discard the liquid.

Cut the pears lengthwise into halves and remove the core using a melon baller or small spoon. Arrange the pears cut side down in a shallow baking dish just large enough to hold the pears. Pour the water and apple juice over the pears and drizzle with the honey.

Bake, loosely covered with foil, in a preheated 375-degree oven for 30 to 35 minutes or until tender. Spread the granola in a shallow baking dish or round baking dish and toast in the oven for 10 minutes while the pears are baking.

At the end of the baking process for the pears, pour the pear baking liquid into a small saucepan. Cook over medium heat until the liquid is reduced to 1/4 cup and of a syrup consistency. Divide the yogurt evenly between four shallow bowls and place one warm pear half cut side up in each bowl. Sprinkle evenly with the granola and drizzle with the syrup. Garnish each serving with a fresh mint leaf. Serve immediately. *Yield: 4 servings.*

FLAN

- $1\frac{1}{2}$ cups sugar
- 1 (14-ounce) can sweetened condensed milk
- 14 ounces milk (use condensed milk can to measure)
- 8 ounces cream cheese
- 6 eggs
- $1\frac{1}{2}$ teaspoons vanilla extract

Heat the sugar in a small saucepan over medium-high heat until caramelized or until the sugar melts and browns, stirring with a spoon to prevent clumping if necessary. Pour the caramelized sugar into an 8-inch baking pan or baking dish, tilting the pan to ensure even coverage over the bottom and over a small portion of the side of the pan.

Combine the condensed milk, milk, cream cheese, eggs and vanilla in a blender and process until blended. Pour the cream cheese mixture over the prepared layer. Place the baking pan in a larger baking pan and pour enough water into the larger pan to come halfway up the side of the smaller pan. Bake in a preheated 350-degree oven for $1\frac{1}{4}$ hours or until a cake tester or thin knife blade inserted in the center comes out clean. Chill, covered, in the refrigerator. The use of low-fat or fat-free cream cheese is not recommended for this recipe.
Yield: 8 servings.

NOTE: For coconut flan, substitute one 14-ounce can cream of coconut for the sweetened condensed milk and reduce the amount of milk to 7 ounces.

FLORIDA DAIRY

Florida is the leading dairy state in the Southeast, producing more than two billion pounds of milk on a yearly average with sales exceeding $430 million. Florida has 175 dairy farms and a herd of 138,000 cows, mostly of the black and white Holstein variety. The industry employs nearly 4,000 people.

Each Florida dairy cow produces more than 2,000 gallons of milk annually. Okeechobee is the leading dairy county in Florida, with nineteen dairies and 33,000 cows. The three leading counties (Okeechobee, Gilchrist, and Hardee) account for more than 43 percent of the state's dairy cows.

Dairy farmers recycle about 170,000 tons of by-products, such as citrus pulp and whole cottonseed, that are consumed by cows instead of ending up in landfills.

Classic Cream Pound Cake

3 cups all-purpose flour
1/8 teaspoon salt
3 cups sugar
1 cup (2 sticks) butter, softened
6 eggs
1 tablespoon vanilla extract
1 cup heavy whipping cream

Sift the flour and salt together. Beat the sugar and butter in a mixing bowl until light and fluffy, scraping the bowl occasionally. Add the eggs one at a time, beating well after each addition. Blend in the vanilla. Add the flour mixture alternately with the whipping cream, beating well after each addition and beginning and ending with the flour.

Spoon the batter into a greased and floured 10-inch tube pan. Place the pan in a cold oven and turn the oven to 325 degrees. Bake for 1 1/4 hours or until the cake tests done. Cool in the pan for 10 minutes. Invert onto a wire rack to cool completely. *Yield: 15 servings.*

Strawberry Yogurt Shortcake

2 1/3 cups baking mix
3 tablespoons sugar
1/2 cup creamy strawberry fat-free yogurt
3 tablespoons butter, melted
1 tablespoon sugar
1 quart fresh strawberries, sliced
1 1/2 cups creamy strawberry fat-free yogurt

Combine the baking mix and 3 tablespoons sugar in a bowl and mix well. Add 1/2 cup yogurt and the butter and stir until a soft dough forms. Place the dough on a hard work surface lightly sprinkled with additional baking mix. Gently roll the baking mix into the dough. Shape the dough into a ball and knead eight to ten times.

Roll the dough 1/2 inch thick and cut into six rounds with a floured 3-inch biscuit cutter. Arrange the rounds on an ungreased baking sheet and sprinkle with 1 tablespoon sugar. Bake in a preheated 450-degree oven for 8 to 10 minutes or until golden brown. Split the shortcakes into halves and place on individual dessert plates. Spoon equal amounts of the strawberries and 1 1/2 cups yogurt between the halves and over the tops. Serve immediately. *Yield: 6 servings.*

Family and Consumer Sciences Programs

Family and Consumer Sciences (FCS) programs empower individuals, families, youth, and communities by providing relevant, responsive, accessible, and inclusive programs that result in positive changes in their lives.

Program areas include all aspects of home, family, and community life: raising children, food and nutrition, healthy lifestyles, housing, home management, family finances, food safety, caregiving, volunteer program development, community development, and more.

FCS educators offer programs to develop parenting skills in all families. Many of our programs target audiences in greater need of information and skills to care for and guide their children such as single parents, teen parents, divorced parents, kinship caregivers, incarcerated parents, and parents that are court ordered to attend parenting programs because of child abuse and neglect. Though adapted to the needs of the different audiences, every program helps parents develop skills to better care for and guide their children.

The commitment to young people does not stop with their parents. FCS programs also include youth development programs offered through schools, Extension offices, 4-H, and the After School Enrichment Project. These range in subject matter from skills for independent living to leadership development.

Promoting healthy lifestyles comprises another keystone of FCS programs. Food, nutrition, and health programs focus on healthy eating, exercise, preventative health care, and behaviors. Programs such as the Expanded Food Nutrition Education Program (EFNEP) teach families the skills they need to adopt a healthy diet. Diabetes nutrition education and programs to train volunteers to be Master Food and Nutrition Educators serve our communities by sharing science-based nutrition education.

Food safety and quality programs encourage safe home food practices, such as hand washing and use of food thermometers, and certify restaurant workers through the ServSafe program.

Educators in leadership development share the skills needed to take leadership roles with individuals across the state. Through our Nonprofit Organization and Leadership Development Program, nonprofit organizations find the help they need in forming and promoting programs to serve the needs of our families and communities.

Our housing faculty provides programs to prepare moderate- and low-income families for homeownership. In addition, programs on how to maintain property values, prevent and abate dangerous moisture and mildew problems, home safety and security, and household maintenance provide residents with the information they need to take the proper measures toward a healthier home environment.

FCS money management programs serve audiences from school-aged children through retirement age. These programs improve participants' quality of life through teaching responsible money management and financial planning. These programs range from money management and consumer skills classes for adolescents to programs that address end-of-life and estate planning issues for older adults. Fraud prevention, understanding insurance, comparison shopping, and savings components of programs additionally serve to shape the financial well-being of low- and moderate-income Floridians and their families, young or old.

Caregiving programs address the housing, safety, financial well-being, and individual and family needs created by our aging population. Medicare Part D programs prepare volunteers and faculty to assist individuals in understanding and enrolling in the proper Medicare Part D prescription programs.

The Family, Youth and Community Sciences undergraduate and graduate degrees are interdisciplinary applied social science programs. These programs prepare students for careers in human services, community development, and youth professions in both the public and private sector and both nonprofit and for-profit organizations.

For more information about Family and Consumer Sciences programs in your area, contact your local County Extension office. For information about University of Florida/IFAS Extension, visit our Web site at www.solutionsforyourlife.com.

Florida Extension Association of Family and Consumer Sciences . . .
Raising Kids, Eating Right, Spending Smart, Living Well.

A Bountiful Harvest of Nuts, Beans & Grains

A Bountiful Harvest of Nuts, Beans & Grains

Curried Pecans

2 tablespoons butter
2 tablespoons vegetable oil
1 1/2 tablespoons curry powder
1 1/2 teaspoons Worcestershire sauce
1/2 teaspoon salt
1/4 teaspoon cayenne pepper
1 pound pecan or walnut halves

Combine the butter, oil, curry powder, Worcestershire sauce, salt and cayenne pepper in a skillet and heat until the butter melts, stirring frequently. Add the pecans to the skillet and stir until coated.

Spread the coated pecans in a single layer on a baking sheet lined with parchment paper. Bake in a preheated 300-degree oven for 10 minutes. Turn off the oven and let the pecans stand in the oven with the door closed until cool. Store in an airtight container. *Yield: 10 servings.*

Spiced Pecans

1 egg white
1 teaspoon cold water
1 pound pecan halves
1/2 cup sugar
1/2 teaspoon ground cinnamon
1/4 teaspoon salt

Beat the egg white with the cold water in a mixing bowl until frothy. Add the pecans and stir until coated. Mix the sugar, cinnamon and salt in a bowl and stir into the pecan mixture.

Spread the coated pecans in a single layer on a buttered 10×15-inch baking pan. Bake in a preheated 225-degree oven for 1 hour, stirring every 15 minutes. Let stand until cool. Store in an airtight container. *Yield: 10 servings.*

Sweet and Salty Pecans

$3^1/_2$ tablespoons lightly salted butter
$^1/_2$ cup sugar
$^1/_8$ teaspoon cayenne pepper
3 cups pecan halves
1 teaspoon coarse salt

Melt the butter in a heavy skillet over medium heat. Stir in the sugar and cayenne pepper. Increase the heat to high and cook for 1 minute, stirring constantly. Stir in the pecans and reduce the heat to medium.

Cook until the pecans are rich brown in color, stirring constantly. Spread the pecans on a baking sheet and sprinkle with the salt, tossing occasionally until cool. Store in an airtight container. *Yield: 6 servings.*

Pecan Pie

1 cup dark corn syrup
1 cup sugar
3 eggs, lightly beaten
1 tablespoon margarine, melted
1 teaspoon vanilla extract
1 cup pecans
1 unbaked (9-inch) pie shell

Combine the corn syrup, sugar, eggs, margarine and vanilla in a bowl and mix until blended. Stir in the pecans. Spoon into the pie shell. Place the pie shell on an oven rack in the lower third of the oven. Bake in a preheated 350-degree oven for 50 to 55 minutes or until set. *Yield: 8 servings.*

Skillet Cookies

2 cups sugar
1 cup (2 sticks) butter or margarine
2 cups dates, chopped
2 eggs, beaten
6 cups crisp rice cereal
1 cup pecans, chopped
$^1/_2$ cup shredded coconut

Melt the sugar and butter in an electric skillet or cast-iron skillet. Stir in the dates and eggs and cook over medium heat for 5 minutes, stirring constantly. Remove from the heat and stir in the cereal and pecans. Let stand just until cool enough to handle.

Butter your hands and shape the date mixture by teaspoonfuls into small balls. Arrange in a greased dish. Coat with the coconut and store in an airtight container. *Yield: 30 (1-cookie) servings.*

Quick-Mex Bean Dip

1 (5-ounce) can black or white soybeans, cooked
1 tablespoon taco seasoning mix
1 tablespoon salsa

Combine the soybeans, seasoning mix and salsa in a blender and process until smooth, adding additional salsa if needed to reach the desired consistency. Serve chilled or warm with tortilla chips. *Yield: 10 servings.*

EDAMAME

Edamame are green soybeans harvested just prior to their maturity. Cooked and lightly salted, these little green beans are a popular snack. They are often sold in the freezer section of your local supermarket either shelled or in the pods. Edamame are a complete protein source, and also provide fiber, essential fatty acids, and isoflavones. A 3/4-cup serving provides 60 calories, 7 grams of carbohydrate, 1.5 grams of fat, and 4 grams of protein.

Spicy Roasted Garlic and Soybean Dip

6 unpeeled garlic cloves
Salt to taste
1 (16-ounce) package frozen soybeans (edamame)
1 1/4 teaspoons salt
1/2 teaspoon ground coriander
1/2 teaspoon cayenne pepper
1/4 teaspoon ground cumin
6 tablespoons olive oil
1/4 cup lime juice

Roast the garlic in an ungreased skillet over medium heat for 15 minutes or until softened, turning frequently. Remove the garlic to a platter to cool. Peel the garlic and place the garlic cloves in a bowl.

Bring enough water to cover the soybeans and salt to a boil in a saucepan and add the soybeans. Boil for 5 minutes. Drain, reserving the soybeans and 1 cup of the cooking liquid. Cool the soybeans to room temperature.

Combine the soybeans, garlic, 1 1/4 teaspoons salt, the coriander, cayenne pepper and cumin in a blender and pulse to combine. Add 1/2 to 3/4 cup of the reserved cooking liquid and process until puréed. Add the olive oil and lime juice and pulse until combined. Serve with chips and/or assorted party crackers. *Yield: 10 servings.*

Suwannee County Black Bean Soup

- 1 onion, chopped
- 1/2 cup chopped green bell pepper
- 2 teaspoons olive oil
- 3 garlic cloves, chopped
- 1 tablespoon chili powder
- 1 teaspoon ground cumin
- 1/2 teaspoon oregano
- 3 (15-ounce) cans black beans (1 can drained)
- 1/2 teaspoon pepper (optional)

Mix the onion, bell pepper and olive oil in a microwave-safe bowl and microwave for 2 minutes. Combine the onion mixture, garlic, chili powder, cumin and oregano in a stockpot and mix well.

Purée one undrained can of the beans in a food processor and stir into the stockpot. Add the remaining two cans of beans (one drained and one undrained) to the stockpot and mix well. Bring to a boil and reduce the heat to low.

Simmer for 25 minutes, stirring frequently. Season with the pepper and ladle into soup bowls. Top with salsa, shredded cheese and/or additional chopped onion, if desired. *Yield: 6 servings.*

Slow-Cooker Beans and Sausage

- 1 1/2 pounds smoked turkey sausage, sliced
- 1 (15-ounce) can white kidney beans (cannellini) or white navy beans
- 1 (15-ounce) can black beans or chili beans, drained and rinsed
- 1 (15-ounce) can red kidney beans, drained and rinsed
- 1 (15-ounce) can small lima beans, drained and rinsed
- 3 cups frozen whole kernel corn
- 3 cups bottled salsa
- 1 cup chopped green bell pepper
- 1 large onion, chopped
- 1 tablespoon garlic salt
- 1 teaspoon ground cumin, or 3 bay leaves

Combine the sausage, undrained white beans, black beans, kidney beans, lima beans, corn, salsa, bell pepper, onion, garlic salt and cumin in a 3 1/2- to 4-quart slow cooker and mix well. Cook, covered, on Low for 6 to 7 hours, or on High for 3 to 3 1/2 hours. *Yield: 6 servings.*

Peanut Butter Squares

2 cups (4 sticks) butter, softened
1/3 (16-ounce) package graham crackers, crushed
1 cup peanut butter
3 1/2 cups confectioners' sugar
2 cups (12 ounces) semisweet chocolate chips

Combine the butter, graham cracker crumbs, peanut butter and confectioners' sugar in a bowl and mix well. Press over the bottom of a greased 10×15-inch baking pan.

Melt the chocolate chips in a double boiler over hot water or in the microwave. Spread the melted chocolate over the prepared layer and chill until firm. Cut into 2×2-inch squares. *Yield: 35 (2×2-inch-square) servings.*

Frozen Peanut Butter Pie

4 ounces cream cheese, softened
1 cup confectioners' sugar
1/3 cup peanut butter
1/2 cup milk
9 ounces whipped topping
1 baked (9-inch) pie shell, cooled
1/4 cup finely chopped peanuts

Beat the cream cheese in a mixing bowl until light and fluffy. Add the confectioners' sugar and peanut butter and beat until blended. Add the milk gradually, beating constantly until smooth. Fold in the whipped topping.

Spoon the peanut butter mixture into the pie shell and sprinkle with the peanuts. Freeze until firm. You may substitute a graham cracker pie shell for the baked pie shell. *Yield: 6 servings.*

Peanut Butter Zebras

6 tablespoons butter, softened
3/4 teaspoon salt
1/2 teaspoon baking powder
1 1/2 cups all-purpose flour
1 cup packed brown sugar
1/3 cup shortening
1/2 cup peanut butter
1 egg
1/2 teaspoon vanilla extract
48 Hershey's Hugs®

Beat the butter, salt and baking powder in a mixing bowl until blended. Add the flour 1/2 cup at a time, beating constantly until fine crumbs form and scraping the bowl frequently. Add the brown sugar, shortening, peanut butter, egg and vanilla and beat until blended.

Shape the dough into 1-inch balls and arrange 2 inches apart on an ungreased cookie sheet. Bake in a preheated 375-degree oven for 9 to 12 minutes or until light golden brown. Immediately top each warm cookie with one of the candies and press the candies into the cookies until the edges slightly crack. Remove to a wire rack to cool completely. Store in an airtight container. *Yield: 48 (1-cookie) servings.*

Microwave Soy Nut Brittle

1 cup sugar
1/2 cup light corn syrup
1 cup roasted soybeans
1 teaspoon margarine
1 teaspoon vanilla extract
1 teaspoon baking soda

Measure all the ingredients in advance and lightly grease a baking sheet. Combine the sugar and corn syrup in a 1/2-quart microwave-safe baking dish. Microwave on High for 4 minutes. Stir in the soybeans and microwave on High for 3 to 5 minutes or until light brown in color. Stir in the margarine and vanilla.

Microwave on High for 1 to 2 minutes longer. The soybeans will be light brown in color and the syrup will be very hot. Add the baking soda gradually, stirring constantly until light and foamy. Make sure this step is accomplished quickly or the brittle will become too cool to pour. Pour the brittle mixture onto the prepared baking sheet and cool for 30 to 60 minutes. Break into small pieces and store in an airtight container. *Yield: 16 servings.*

Barley Casserole

1/2 cup (1 stick) margarine
1 cup quick-cooking fine barley
1 onion, chopped
2 cups chicken broth
1 (5-ounce) can water chestnuts, drained and chopped
1 (3-ounce) can mushroom slices, drained
1/2 cup slivered almonds
1 envelope onion soup mix

Melt the margarine in a saucepan and stir in the barley and onion. Sauté just until light golden brown. Add the broth, water chestnuts, mushrooms, almonds and soup mix and mix well.

Spoon the barley mixture into a 2-quart baking dish. Bake, covered, in a preheated 350-degree oven for 1 hour. Add additional broth if needed to reach the desired consistency. *Yield: 6 servings.*

Corn Fritters

1 cup all-purpose flour
1 teaspoon sugar
1 teaspoon baking powder
1/2 teaspoon salt
1/4 cup milk
2 eggs, beaten
1 tablespoon butter, melted
1 1/2 cups fresh or frozen corn
Vegetable oil for deep-frying

Sift the flour, sugar, baking powder and salt into a bowl and mix well. Add the milk, eggs and butter and mix well. Stir in the corn.

Drop the corn mixture by spoonfuls into preheated 365-degree oil in a deep-fryer and fry until golden brown. Drain on paper towels and serve immediately. *Yield: 18 corn fritters.*

The nutritional profile does not include the oil for frying.

Corn Bread Casserole

1 egg, beaten
1 cup sour cream
1/2 cup (1 stick) butter, melted
1 (8-ounce) can corn
1 (8-ounce) can cream-style corn
1 (8-ounce) package corn muffin mix

Combine the egg, sour cream, butter, undrained corn, cream-style corn and muffin mix in the order listed in a bowl and mix well.

Spoon the corn bread mixture into a greased 9×9-inch baking dish. Bake in a preheated 350-degree oven for 40 to 55 minutes or until a wooden pick inserted in the center comes out clean. Serve hot. *Yield: 8 servings.*

Corn Bread Dressing

4 cups crumbled corn bread
2 cups crumbled dry bread
1 large onion, chopped
$1/2$ cup thinly sliced celery
3 eggs, beaten
3 tablespoons parsley flakes
$1\frac{1}{2}$ teaspoons poultry seasoning
1 teaspoon salt
Pepper to taste
2 cups hot chicken broth
$1/2$ cup (1 stick) butter, melted

Combine the corn bread, dry bread, onion, celery, eggs, parsley flakes, poultry seasoning, salt and pepper in a bowl and mix well. Add the broth and butter and stir until moistened. Spoon the corn bread mixture into a 9×13-inch baking dish. Bake in a preheated 350-degree oven for 45 minutes. *Yield: 10 servings.*

Grits Casserole

8 ounces sausage, cooked and drained
1 cup leftover grits
$1/2$ cup milk
1 egg
2 to 3 tablespoons butter
Salt and pepper to taste
$1/2$ cup (2 ounces) shredded Cheddar cheese

Spoon the sausage into a 2-quart baking dish coated with nonstick cooking spray. Combine the grits, milk, egg, butter, salt and pepper in a blender and process for a few seconds until blended. Add cheese and pulse just until combined.

Spread the grits mixture over the sausage. Bake in a preheated 350-degree oven for 30 minutes or until the edges are brown. *Yield: 4 servings.*

Walnut Fried Rice

- 1 1/2 teaspoons vegetable oil
- 2 eggs, beaten
- 1 tablespoon vegetable oil
- 1/2 cup chopped walnuts
- 12 ounces boneless skinless chicken breasts, thinly sliced
- Pepper to taste
- 1 cup sliced fresh mushrooms
- 1 cup edamame or green peas
- 1/2 cup thinly sliced carrots
- 1/4 cup thinly sliced green onions
- 1 teaspoon grated fresh ginger, or 1/2 teaspoon ground ginger
- 3 cups cooked brown rice, chilled
- 2 tablespoons low-sodium soy sauce

Heat 1 1/2 teaspoons oil in a large skillet or wok over medium heat until hot. Add the eggs and cook until set; do not stir. Invert the skillet over a baking sheet to remove the eggs. Slice the eggs into thin strips.

Heat 1 tablespoon oil in the same skillet or wok over medium-high heat until hot. Add the walnuts and stir-fry until light brown. Sprinkle the chicken with pepper and add the chicken to the skillet. Stir-fry for 2 to 3 minutes or until cooked through. Stir in the mushrooms, edamame, carrots, green onions and ginger and stir-fry for 3 minutes. Stir in the rice and eggs. Sprinkle with the soy sauce and toss until combined. Serve immediately. *Yield: 6 servings.*

NOTE: To save time, use quick-cooking brown rice.

STAYING REGULAR

It may be a topic we do not like to discuss in "polite company," but staying regular is important to all of us, especially as we get older. To keep our gastrointestinal tracts in good shape we should eat a fiber-rich diet, drink an adequate amount of water, and stay active.

For a fiber-rich diet, enjoy a variety of fruits, vegetables, legumes, and whole grain foods. Whole grains contain all three parts of the grain: germ, endosperm, and bran. Bran contains fiber, and the germ is a good source of vitamins and minerals. As you increase dietary fiber, drink extra fluids, especially water, to help you avoid unpleasant side effects.

Delicious Stove-Top Rice Pudding

3 cups milk
1 cup water
1/2 cup rice
1/2 cup sugar
Grated zest of 1 lemon
Ground cinnamon to taste

Combine the milk, water, rice, sugar and lemon zest in a large saucepan and mix well. Bring to a boil and reduce the heat to low.

Simmer until the liquid is almost absorbed and the rice is tender, stirring frequently. Spoon the pudding into individual dessert bowls and sprinkle with cinnamon. Serve warm or chilled. *Yield: 6 servings.*

Cuban Bread

1/2 cup warm water
2 tablespoons sugar
4 envelopes dry yeast
1 1/2 cups warm water
2 teaspoons salt
7 to 8 cups unbleached flour
Cornmeal

Mix 1/2 cup warm water and the sugar in a large bowl. Sprinkle the yeast over the sugar mixture and let stand for 5 minutes or until foamy. Stir in 1 1/2 cups warm water and the salt. Add the flour 1 cup at a time, stirring with a wooden spoon until the dough forms a ball.

Knead the dough on a lightly floured surface for 7 minutes or until the dough feels satiny. Cover the dough with the mixing bowl and let rise for 15 minutes or until doubled in bulk. Punch the dough down and divide into two equal portions. Shape each portion into a slightly flattened loaf.

Arrange the loaves on a baking sheet lightly sprinkled with cornmeal. Make an X in the top of each loaf. Place the baking sheet in a cold oven and turn the oven to 350 degrees. Bake for 40 to 50 minutes or until golden brown. Serve warm. Store leftover bread in sealable plastic bags. *Yield: 10 servings.*

Health Bread

- $7\frac{1}{2}$ to $8\frac{1}{2}$ cups unbleached flour
- 1 cup whole wheat flour
- 1 tablespoon salt
- 2 envelopes dry yeast
- $1\frac{1}{2}$ cups cottage cheese
- 1 cup rolled oats
- 1 cup whole bran cereal
- $\frac{1}{2}$ cup molasses
- 2 tablespoons margarine
- $2\frac{1}{2}$ cups boiling water
- $\frac{3}{4}$ cup chopped walnuts
- $\frac{3}{4}$ cup chopped dates
- $\frac{3}{4}$ cup raisins

Combine 1 cup of the unbleached flour, the whole wheat flour, salt and yeast in a large mixing bowl and mix well. Combine the cottage cheese, oats, cereal, molasses and margarine in a heatproof bowl and mix well. Stir in the boiling water. Cool to 120 degrees.

Add the cottage cheese mixture gradually to the flour mixture, beating constantly for 2 minutes. Add enough of the remaining unbleached flour to make a soft dough and mix well. Knead for 10 minutes.

Place the dough in a greased bowl, turning to coat. Let rise for 45 minutes or until doubled in bulk. Punch the dough down and invert onto a lightly floured surface. Knead in the walnuts, dates and raisins.

Divide the dough into three equal portions and shape each portion into a loaf in a 5×9-inch loaf pan. Let rise, covered with tea towels, for 45 minutes or until doubled in bulk. Bake in a preheated 375-degree oven for 35 to 45 minutes or until the loaves test done. Cool in the pans for 10 minutes and remove to a wire rack to cool completely. Cut each loaf into eight thick slices. *Yield: 24 (1-slice) servings.*

FRUIT PURÉES

Many of Florida's fruits can be puréed for use in all types of recipes. This simply means using a food processor to liquefy the fruit, sometimes including the peel. The fruits usually contain enough liquid that a pourable thick purée will result. Add the purée to sauces, to batters for making breads and muffins, use as a marinade, or as a salad dressing. Be creative in using Florida fruit purées to enhance your cooking imagination.

KUMQUAT BANANA NUT BREAD

3 cups all-purpose flour
2 cups sugar
1 teaspoon baking soda
1 teaspoon salt
1 teaspoon ground cinnamon
1 cup chopped pecans
2 cups mashed bananas
1 cup vegetable oil
2/3 cup kumquat purée (about 30 kumquats)
3 eggs, beaten
2 teaspoons vanilla extract

Combine the flour, sugar, baking soda, salt and cinnamon in a bowl and mix well. Stir in the pecans. Mix the bananas, oil, purée, eggs and vanilla in a bowl. Add the banana mixture to the flour mixture and stir just until moistened.

Pour the batter evenly into two greased and floured 5×9-inch loaf pans. Bake in a preheated 350-degree oven for 65 minutes or until the loaves test done. Cool in the pans for 10 minutes and remove to a wire rack to cool completely. Cut each loaf into eight slices. *Yield: 16 (1-slice) servings.*

MANGO NUT BREAD

1 3/4 cups all-purpose flour, sifted
2 teaspoons baking powder
1/4 teaspoon baking soda
2/3 cup sugar
1/3 cup shortening
2 eggs
1 cup mashed mango
1/2 cup pecans, chopped
1/2 cup raisins

Sift the flour, baking powder and baking soda together. Beat the sugar and shortening in a mixing bowl until creamy. Add the eggs and beat until fluffy. Add the flour mixture alternately with the mango, beating until smooth after each addition. Stir in the pecans and raisins.

Spoon the batter into a greased 5×9-inch loaf pan. Bake in a preheated 350-degree oven for 1 hour or until a knife inserted in the center of the loaf comes out clean. Cool in the pan for 10 minutes. Remove to a wire rack to cool completely. *Yield: 8 servings.*

Whole Wheat Banana Bread

- 1 cup all-purpose flour
- 1 cup whole wheat flour
- 1 teaspoon baking soda
- 1 teaspoon salt
- 3 large ripe bananas, mashed
- 3/4 cup sugar
- 1 egg, lightly beaten
- 2 tablespoons butter, melted
- 1/4 cup milk

Sift the all-purpose flour, whole wheat flour, baking soda and salt together. Combine the bananas, sugar and egg in a bowl and mix well. Stir in the butter. Add the flour mixture to the banana mixture and mix well. Stir in the milk.

Spoon the batter into a greased 5×9-inch loaf pan. Bake in a preheated 350-degree oven for 1 hour. Cool in the pan for 10 minutes. Remove to a wire rack to cool completely. *Yield: 10 servings.*

Whole Wheat Dinner Rolls

- 2 envelopes dry yeast
- 1 cup warm water
- 2 cups hot water
- 3/4 cup vegetable oil
- 1/4 cup honey
- 2 eggs, beaten
- 2 teaspoons sea salt
- 6 cups whole wheat flour

Dissolve the yeast in the warm water in a large bowl. Add the hot water, oil, honey, eggs and sea salt and mix well. Add the whole wheat flour gradually, mixing well after each addition; do not knead.

Place the dough in a large greased bowl, turning to coat the surface. Chill, covered with plastic wrap, for 8 to 10 hours. Stir down the dough. Shape the dough by 1/4-cupfuls into rolls and arrange the rolls in two greased 9×13-inch baking pans. Bake in a preheated 425-degree oven for 10 to 13 minutes or until golden brown. *Yield: 24 rolls.*

FINDING WHOLE GRAINS

Whole grains provide dietary fiber and a variety of vitamins and minerals that are lost when grains are processed. You can identify foods made with whole grains by reading the ingredient list on food labels. Ingredients are listed in order by weight, so look for a whole grain as the first ingredient. Whole grains available in the United States include:

whole wheat
whole oats/oatmeal
whole grain corn
popcorn
brown rice
whole rye
whole grain barley
wild rice
buckwheat/kasha
triticale
bulgur (cracked wheat)
millet
quinoa
sorghum

Be adventurous and try new grains for variety!

Oatmeal Pancakes

2 cups buttermilk
1 1/2 cups old-fashioned oats
1/2 cup sifted all-purpose flour
1 teaspoon salt
1 teaspoon sugar
1 teaspoon baking soda
2 eggs, beaten

Combine the buttermilk and oats in a bowl and mix well. Stir in the flour, salt, sugar, baking soda and eggs.

Pour 1/3 cup of the batter per pancake onto a preheated lightly oiled griddle. Cook until bubbles appear on the surface and the underside is golden brown. Turn the pancake and cook until the remaining side is golden brown. Repeat the process with the remaining batter. Serve with cane syrup. *Yield: 4 servings.*

Granola

3 cups rolled oats
1/2 cup raisins
1/2 cup sweetened dried cranberries
1/2 cup sliced almonds
1/2 cup chopped pecans
1/2 cup nonfat dry milk powder
1/2 cup wheat germ
1/3 cup sunflower seeds
1/4 cup sesame seeds
1/4 cup sugar, or equivalent amount of artificial sweetener
1/4 cup unsweetened coconut
1 teaspoon ground cinnamon
1/4 teaspoon salt
1/2 cup canola oil
1/4 cup honey

Combine the oats, raisins, cranberries, almonds, pecans, dry milk powder, wheat germ, sunflower seeds, sesame seeds, sugar, coconut, cinnamon and salt in a bowl and mix well. Add the canola oil and honey and stir until coated.

Spread the oats mixture on a large baking sheet sprayed with nonstick cooking spray. Bake in a preheated 250-degree oven for 30 minutes, stirring every 10 minutes. Let stand until cool and store in an airtight container. *Yield: 14 servings.*

Sun-Ripened Fruits

Sun-Ripened Fruits

Microwave Bananas Foster

- 3/4 cup (1 1/2 sticks) margarine
- 3/4 cup packed brown sugar
- 6 tablespoons dark rum
- 2 tablespoons banana liqueur
- 1/8 teaspoon ground cinnamon
- 6 small firm bananas

Combine the margarine and brown sugar in a 6×10-inch microwave-safe dish and cover with waxed paper. Microwave on High for 1 1/2 to 2 minutes, stirring after 1 minute. Stir in the rum, liqueur and cinnamon.

Cut the bananas lengthwise into halves and then cut each half crosswise into halves. Arrange the bananas cut side down in the rum mixture and cover with waxed paper. Microwave on High for 45 to 60 seconds or until hot. Turn the bananas and baste with the rum mixture.

Microwave, covered with waxed paper, on High for 45 to 60 seconds longer or until the bananas are heated through. Serve immediately over vanilla ice cream or frozen yogurt in dessert bowls. *Yield: 6 servings.*

POTASSIUM AND BLOOD PRESSURE

Fruits and vegetables are packed with vitamins and minerals. One mineral found in many fruits and vegetables is potassium. It has many functions in our bodies, and is of interest today for its role in reducing the risk for high blood pressure.

Good sources of potassium include bananas, leafy greens, potatoes, melons, oranges or orange juice, and root vegetables such as carrots and beets. Eating these foods is especially important for people who take diuretic medications that cause potassium to be lost in the urine along with excess water and sodium. Check with your health care provider to see if your medications cause potassium loss.

Blueberry Buckle

2 cups sifted all-purpose flour
2 1/2 teaspoons baking powder
1/2 teaspoon salt
1/4 cup packed light brown sugar
3 tablespoons all-purpose flour
1/2 teaspoon ground cinnamon
2 tablespoons butter or margarine
1/2 cup granulated sugar
1/4 cup (1/2 stick) butter or margarine, softened
1 egg, lightly beaten
1/2 cup milk
2 cups fresh or frozen blueberries

Sift 2 cups flour, the baking powder and salt together. Combine the brown sugar, 3 tablespoons flour and the cinnamon in a bowl and mix well. Cut 2 tablespoons butter into the brown sugar mixture until crumbly.

Beat the granulated sugar, 1/4 cup butter and the egg in a mixing bowl until light and fluffy. Add the flour mixture alternately with the milk, beating well after each addition. Stir in 1/2 cup of the blueberries.

Spoon the blueberry mixture into a greased 8×8-inch baking dish and top with the remaining 1 1/2 cups blueberries. Sprinkle with the brown sugar mixture and bake in a preheated 350-degree oven for 1 hour or until the edges pull from the sides of the dish. Cool in the baking dish on a wire rack for 5 minutes. Run a sharp knife around the edges to loosen and cut into nine squares. Serve warm. *Yield: 9 servings.*

Fruit Cobbler

1 (28-ounce) can sliced peaches, drained
1 (28-ounce) can pears
1 cup fresh or frozen blueberries
3 cups applesauce
2 cups baking mix
1 tablespoon sugar

Combine the peaches, undrained pears and blueberries in a bowl and mix gently. Stir in 2 cups of the applesauce. Spoon the fruit mixture into a 9×13-inch baking pan.

Mix the remaining 1 cup applesauce and the baking mix in a bowl and pour over the fruit mixture. Sprinkle with the sugar and bake in a preheated 375-degree oven for 35 to 45 minutes or until brown and bubbly. *Yield: 10 servings.*

Blueberry Dessert

1 (21-ounce) can blueberry pie filling
1 (25-ounce) jar applesauce
1 (9-ounce) package yellow cake mix
1/2 cup pecans, chopped
2 teaspoons ground cinnamon
1/4 cup (1/2 stick) margarine, melted

Mix the pie filling and applesauce in a round 3-quart microwave-safe dish. Sprinkle with the cake mix, pecans and cinnamon. Drizzle with the margarine.

Microwave on High for 12 to 15 minutes, turning the dish one-fourth after 6 minutes. Let stand for 30 minutes before serving. Serve alone or spoon over ice cream, pound cake or angel food cake. *Yield: 8 servings.*

NOTE: Keep these ingredients on hand for a great last minute dessert.

Blueberry-Filled Dutch Pancake

1 tablespoon margarine
1/2 cup fat-free or low-fat milk
3 eggs
1/3 cup all-purpose flour
3 tablespoons sugar
1 1/2 cups fresh blueberries or drained thawed frozen blueberries
1/4 teaspoon ground cinnamon
1/2 cup sliced banana

Melt the margarine in a 9-inch baking dish and tilt to coat evenly. Whisk the fat-free milk and eggs in a bowl until blended. Add the flour and 1 tablespoon of the sugar and whisk until smooth. Pour the batter into the prepared baking dish and bake in a preheated 450-degree oven for 8 minutes. Reduce the heat to 375 degrees and bake for 8 to 10 minutes longer or until the sides of the pancake are puffy and the top is golden brown.

Combine the remaining 2 tablespoons sugar, the blueberries and cinnamon in a bowl and mix gently. Scatter the banana over the top of the pancake and spoon the blueberry mixture over the banana. Cut into wedges and serve immediately. *Yield: 4 servings.*

NOTE: When doubling the recipe, bake in a 9×13-inch baking pan in a preheated 425-degree oven for 20 to 25 minutes.

Blueberry Gelatin Salad

2 (3-ounce) packages grape gelatin
2 cups boiling water
1 (20-ounce) can crushed pineapple
1 (16-ounce) can blueberry pie filling
8 ounces cream cheese, softened
1 cup sour cream
1/2 cup sugar
1 teaspoon vanilla extract
1/2 cup chopped pecans

Mix the gelatin and boiling water in heatproof bowl until the gelatin dissolves. Let stand until slightly thickened and stir in the undrained pineapple and pie filling. Pour the gelatin mixture into a 9×13-inch dish.

Combine the cream cheese, sour cream, sugar and vanilla in a mixing bowl and beat until blended. Spread the cream cheese mixture over the top of the gelatin mixture and sprinkle with the pecans. Chill, covered, until set. *Yield: 12 servings.*

Blueberry Pie

- 1 1/2 cups all-purpose flour
- 3/4 cup (1 1/2 sticks) butter, melted
- 1 cup pecans, chopped
- 1 cup sugar
- 8 ounces cream cheese
- 8 ounces whipped topping
- 2 bananas, sliced
- 1 (21-ounce) can blueberry pie filling, chilled

Combine the flour and butter in a bowl and mix well. Stir in the pecans. Press the pecan mixture over the bottom of a 9×13-inch baking dish. Bake in a preheated 350-degree oven for 12 to 15 minutes or until light brown. Cool for 15 to 20 minutes. Beat the sugar and cream cheese in a mixing bowl until creamy. Fold the cream cheese mixture into the whipped topping in a bowl. Spread the cream cheese mixture over the baked layer and top with the bananas. Chill, covered, for 8 to 12 hours. Spread with the pie filling just before serving. Cut into squares to serve. *Yield: 16 servings.*

Crustless Blueberry Pie

- 3 cups fresh or frozen unsweetened blueberries
- 1/3 cup sugar
- 3 tablespoons all-purpose flour
- 1/2 teaspoon grated lemon zest
- 1/2 teaspoon ground cinnamon
- 1/2 teaspoon ground nutmeg
- 1/2 cup quick-cooking oats
- 2 tablespoons brown sugar
- 1/2 teaspoon ground cinnamon
- 1 1/2 tablespoons firm margarine

If using frozen blueberries place in a microwave-safe 8-cup measure and microwave on High for 2 to 3 minutes. Combine the blueberries, sugar, flour, lemon zest, 1/2 teaspoon cinnamon and the nutmeg in a large bowl and mix gently. Pour the blueberry mixture into an 8- or 9-inch microwave-safe pie plate.

Mix the oats, brown sugar and 1/2 teaspoon cinnamon in a bowl. Cut the margarine into the oats mixture using a pastry blender or two knives until crumbly. Sprinkle the crumb mixture over the blueberry mixture and microwave on High for 5 minutes. Microwave on Medium for 3 to 5 minutes or until bubbly and thick. Serve warm. *Yield: 8 servings.*

Blueberry Strata

1 (24-inch) baguette French bread
3 cups fat-free milk
3/4 cup packed brown sugar
6 eggs
1 teaspoon vanilla extract
1/2 teaspoon ground cinnamon
2 cups blueberries
1 cup pecans, toasted
1/4 cup packed brown sugar
1/4 cup (1/2 stick) margarine or butter, melted

Cut the baguette into twenty 1-inch slices. Arrange the slices in a single layer in a 9×13-inch baking dish. Whisk the fat-free milk, 3/4 cup brown sugar, the eggs, vanilla and cinnamon in a bowl until blended and pour over the bread. Chill, covered with plastic wrap, for 8 to 24 hours.

Remove the baking dish from the refrigerator and top the chilled layer with the blueberries and pecans. Sprinkle with 1/4 cup brown sugar and drizzle with the margarine. Bake in a preheated 400-degree oven for 20 to 30 minutes or until brown and bubbly. Drizzle with maple syrup or blueberry syrup, if desired, and serve immediately. *Yield: 12 servings.*

FLORIDA FRUIT CUP

Keep these ingredients on hand in the refrigerator for a quick dessert or handy snack. Mix 1 cup pineapple chunks, 1 cup sliced mango, 1 sliced banana and 1 cup orange juice in a bowl. Chill, covered, in the refrigerator. Sprinkle with fresh grated coconut or packaged shredded coconut. Garnish each serving with guava jelly just before serving. Yield: 6 (1/2-cup) servings.

Fresh Berry-Stuffed French Toast with Yogurt Sauce

8 ounces (2 cups) mixed fresh blueberries,
strawberries, raspberries or blackberries
2 tablespoons confectioners' sugar
1/3 cup fat-free sweetened condensed milk
3/4 cup vanilla low-fat yogurt
1 (10-ounce) loaf French bread
1/3 cup low-fat milk
1 egg
1 egg white
1 teaspoon granulated sugar
1 teaspoon vanilla extract
1/4 teaspoon ground cinnamon

Place the berries in a bowl and sprinkle with the confectioners' sugar. Combine about one-fourth of the berry mixture, the condensed milk and yogurt in a blender or food processor and process until puréed. Set aside.

Cut the bread into twelve 1 1/2-inch slices. Make a slit in the side of each slice of bread, cutting to but not through to create a pocket. Stuff the pockets with the remaining berry mixture and press lightly to seal. Reserve any remaining berry mixture for the topping.

Whisk the low-fat milk, egg, egg white, granulated sugar, vanilla and cinnamon in a bowl until blended. Dip the stuffed bread slices in the milk mixture to coat. Cook in a preheated large nonstick skillet over medium heat until light brown on both sides, turning once. Spoon one-sixth of the berry purée onto each of six serving plates. Arrange two slices of French toast and any remaining berry mixture on each plate. *Yield: 6 servings.*

Calamondin Cake

Cake

1 (2-layer) package yellow cake mix
1 (3-ounce) package lemon gelatin
1/3 cup milk
4 eggs, beaten
1 cup calamondin purée
3/4 cup vegetable oil
1 teaspoon lemon extract

Calamondin Icing

2 cups confectioners' sugar
1/2 cup calamondin purée
1/4 cup (1/2 stick) butter or margarine
2 tablespoons lemon juice
1/4 teaspoon salt

To prepare the cake, combine the cake mix and gelatin in a bowl and mix well. Stir in the milk. Add the eggs and mix until blended. Stir in the purée, oil and flavoring. Spoon the batter into a nonstick loaf pan and bake in a preheated 350-degree oven for 45 minutes. Maintain the oven temperature.

To prepare the icing, combine the confectioners' sugar, purée, butter, lemon juice and salt in a mixing bowl and beat until blended. Spread the icing over the top of the hot cake and bake for 5 minutes longer. *Yield: 8 servings.*

CALAMONDIN

The calamondin is a small orange fruit, shaped like a small tangerine. Very acidic, this fruit can be used in beverages, in cooking, and as a seasoning. It preserves well and makes a good marmalade. To use, harvest the fruit when bright orange to avoid tearing the peel, rinse, cut, and remove the seeds. Suggested uses include: serving halves with plates of seafood; garnishing punches, teas, ginger ale, and/or salads with thin slices; juicing and using in place of lemons or limes in a delicious beverage; and mixing with kumquats to make preserves.

USING FLORIDA FIGS

The delicate, sweet flavor of fresh figs is a delight to most Floridians. Whether served as a breakfast fruit, an appetizer, a salad, or a dessert, figs are sure to be a summertime treat. For variety, add chopped figs to your favorite bread or rice stuffing mixture.

Fresh figs are highly perishable. Figs can be kept for up to 1 week by plumping them in sugar syrup. Simply bring 1 cup sugar and 3 cups water to a simmer in a large saucepan. Add rinsed figs gradually and simmer for 10 minutes. Cool and drain well. Arrange the figs in a single layer in a shallow dish and store in the coldest area of the refrigerator.

Crazy Coconut Pie

- 1/2 cup all-purpose flour
- 1/2 teaspoon cream of tartar
- 1/4 teaspoon baking soda
- 4 eggs
- 2 cups milk
- 1 1/2 cups shredded coconut
- 1 cup sugar
- 1/2 cup (1 stick) butter, melted
- 1 teaspoon vanilla extract
- 1/4 teaspoon salt

Sift the flour, cream of tartar and baking soda together. Beat the eggs in a mixing bowl until blended. Add the flour mixture, milk, coconut, sugar, butter, vanilla and salt to the eggs and beat until blended.

Pour into a greased 10-inch pie plate. Bake in a preheated 350-degree oven for 45 minutes or until a knife inserted in the center comes out clean. *Yield: 8 servings.*

Strawberry Fig Preserves

- 3 cups mashed peeled figs
- 3 cups sugar
- 2 (3-ounce) packages strawberry gelatin

Mix the figs, sugar and gelatin in a large saucepan and bring to a boil. Reduce the heat and continue to boil for 3 to 5 minutes, stirring frequently.

Ladle the hot preserves into six hot sterilized 1/2-pint jars, leaving 1/4-inch headspace. Wipe the jar rims and seal with two-piece lids. Process in a boiling water bath for 5 minutes. *Yield: 48 (2-tablespoon) servings.*

Grapefruit Compote in Rosemary Syrup

1 cup sugar
1/2 cup water
1/4 cup honey
3 sprigs of rosemary
12 ounces (6 large) grapefruit
1/2 cup maraschino cherries with stems

Mix the sugar, water, honey and rosemary sprigs in a saucepan and bring to a boil over medium heat. Boil for 5 minutes, stirring occasionally. Remove from the heat and let stand until cool. Discard the rosemary.

Peel, section and seed the grapefruit. Place the grapefruit sections in a bowl. Pour the rosemary syrup over the grapefruit and stir in the cherries. Chill, covered, until serving time. Garnish with additional sprigs of rosemary, if desired. *Yield: 10 servings.*

NOTE: You may substitute 12 ounces oranges for the grapefruit.

FLORIDA BROILED GRAPEFRUIT

Broiled grapefruit makes a great first course for breakfast or any meal. Select a ruby red grapefruit, rinse, and cut into halves. Top each half with 1 tablespoon brown sugar and 1 teaspoon sweetened flaked coconut. Arrange the grapefruit halves in a broiler pan and broil for 3 minutes. Watch carefully as the coconut burns easily. Serve immediately in individual bowls.

To simplify eating, loosen individual sections with a grapefruit knife or paring knife before sprinkling with the brown sugar and coconut.

Kumquat Cake

Cake
$1^1/_2$ cups all-purpose flour
1 teaspoon baking powder
$^1/_2$ teaspoon salt
$^1/_2$ cup (1 stick) butter, softened
1 cup sugar
2 eggs
$^1/_2$ cup milk
2 teaspoons kumquat juice
2 to 3 tablespoons chopped kumquat zest

Kumquat Icing
4 ounces cream cheese, softened
$^1/_4$ cup ($^1/_2$ stick) margarine
$^1/_2$ (16-ounce) package 4X confectioners' sugar, or $2^1/_2$ cups 10X confectioners' sugar
2 teaspoons kumquat juice
$^1/_2$ cup finely chopped pecans

To prepare the cake, mix the flour, baking powder and salt in a bowl. Beat the butter in a mixing bowl until creamy. Add the sugar and beat until light and fluffy. Add the eggs one at a time, beating well after each addition. Add the flour mixture alternately with the milk, beating well after each addition. Stir in the kumquat juice and kumquat zest.

Spoon the batter into a greased and floured 4×8-inch loaf pan and bake in a preheated 350-degree oven for 1 hour or until the cake tests done. Cool in the pan for 10 minutes. Remove to a wire rack to cool completely.

To prepare the icing, beat the cream cheese and margarine in a mixing bowl until creamy. Add the confectioners' sugar and beat until light and fluffy. Mix in the kumquat juice and pecans. Spread the icing over the top and sides of the cake. *Yield: 16 servings.*

Kumquat Flan

1 cup sugar
3 eggs
2 egg yolks
1 1/4 cups sugar
1 (12-ounce) can evaporated milk
1 teaspoon orange extract
1/2 cup kumquat purée

Melt 1 cup sugar in an aluminum saucepan over low heat until liquefied and golden brown in color. Pour the caramelized sugar into a 2-quart glass baking dish or soufflé dish, tilting the dish to ensure even coverage over the bottom and side. Cool on a wire rack.

Combine the eggs and egg yolks in a bowl and stir just until blended; do not beat as this will cause bubbles. Stir in 1 1/4 cups sugar, the evaporated milk and flavoring. Strain the egg mixture into another bowl. Add the purée and mix gently. Pour into the prepared baking dish.

Place the baking dish in a larger baking pan. Add at least one inch of very hot water. Bake in a preheated 350-degree oven for 1 hour or until set and golden in color. Remove to a wire rack to cool.

Chill, covered tightly, for 8 to 10 hours. Invert the flan onto a flat but rimmed serving platter and spoon the caramel sauce over the flan. Garnish with whole kumquats and kumquat leaves. *Yield: 8 servings.*

KUMQUAT

The kumquat is a small, yellow-to-orange skinned citrus fruit with an aromatic peel and tart flesh. The kumquat tree is not only known for its fruit but also for its decorative shrubbery.

Unlike most other citrus fruits that are peeled before eating, both the peel and the flesh of the kumquat are often eaten. This fruit is often used in marmalades and pickles.

Uncooked kumquats add a distinctive flavor to fruit salads. Cooked, they are particularly delicious as a dessert when stewed or used in fruit compotes.

FRUIT ZEST

Recipes often call for lemon, lime, or orange zest. This is made from the peel of the fruit and adds flavor, color, and texture to recipes. The oil in the peel is the source of their powerful flavoring.

Rinse the fruit and using a hand-held grater, grate the outer surface of the fruit being careful to only remove the colored portion of the peel and not the white membrane, which can be bitter.

Zests can be added to sauces, bread batters, icings, and other dishes that will be enhanced by the citrus flavor they impart.

LEMON BARS

1 1/2 cups all-purpose flour, sifted
1/2 cup confectioners' sugar, sifted
3/4 cup (1 1/2 sticks) butter, chilled and cut into tablespoons
3 cups granulated sugar
6 eggs
Grated zest of 3 lemons
1 cup plus 2 tablespoons fresh lemon juice (about 7 lemons)
1/2 cup all-purpose flour
1 cup blanched almonds, toasted and chopped

Combine 1 1/2 cups flour and the confectioners' sugar in a medium bowl and mix well. Cut the butter into the flour mixture with a pastry blender until crumbly. Pat over the bottom of a 9×13-inch baking dish. Bake in a preheated 325-degree oven for 20 to 25 minutes or until golden brown. Cool on a wire rack.

Reduce the oven temperature to 300 degrees. Whisk the granulated sugar and eggs in a bowl until blended. Stir in the lemon zest and lemon juice. Sift in 1/2 cup flour. Add the almonds and mix well.

Pour the lemon filling over the baked layer and bake for 40 minutes or until set. Cool on a wire rack for 1 hour or longer. Dust with additional confectioners' sugar and cut into bars using a sharp knife. *Yield: 3 dozen bars.*

Grandma's Lemon Meringue Pie

5 tablespoons cornstarch
1 1/2 cups water
1 1/2 cups sugar
2 egg yolks, lightly beaten
Grated zest and juice of 2 lemons
1/2 teaspoon salt
1 baked (8-inch) pie shell
2 egg whites
2 tablespoons sugar
1 teaspoon vanilla extract

Dissolve the cornstarch is a small amount of water in a bowl. Bring 1 1/2 cups water and 1 1/2 cups sugar to a boil in a saucepan. Boil until the sugar dissolves. Stir in the cornstarch mixture.

Cook for 3 minutes, stirring frequently. Gradually add the egg yolks, lemon zest, lemon juice and salt to the cornstarch mixture, stirring constantly. Cool slightly and spoon into the pie shell.

Beat the egg whites in a mixing bowl until foamy. Add 2 tablespoons sugar and the vanilla and beat until stiff peaks form. Spread the meringue over the pie filling, spreading to the edge to seal. Bake in a preheated 300-degree oven for 15 minutes.
Yield: 8 servings.

Perfect Lemonade

1 cup superfine sugar
1 cup cold water
$1^1/2$ cups fresh lemon juice
Finely grated zest of 4 lemons
2 quarts cold water

Mix the superfine sugar and 1 cup cold water in a saucepan and bring to a boil. Reduce the heat to low and simmer for 5 minutes until of a syrup consistency. Let stand until cool.

Combine the syrup, lemon juice and lemon zest in a large pitcher or large jar with a tight-fitting lid. Add 2 quarts cold water and stir vigorously. Pour over ice in tall glasses. Garnish with lemon slices and fresh mint leaves. *Yield: 10 servings.*

Easy Key Lime Pie

1 (14-ounce) can sweetened condensed milk
$^1/2$ cup fresh or bottled Key lime juice
8 ounces whipped topping
Yellow food coloring (optional)
1 (9-inch) graham cracker pie shell

Combine the condensed milk and lime juice in a bowl and mix well. Fold in the whipped topping. Blend in one or two drops of yellow food coloring.

Spoon into the pie shell and chill for 2 hours or until firm. Garnish each serving with additional whipped topping and Key lime slices, if desired. The use of nonfat whipped topping is not recommended in this recipe. *Yield: 6 servings.*

Key Lime Pie

1/4 cup (1/2 stick) margarine
1 1/4 cups graham cracker crumbs
1/3 cup sugar
1/2 cup egg substitute (equivalent to 4 eggs)
2 (14-ounce) cans sweetened condensed milk
1/2 cup Key lime juice
8 ounces whipped topping

Place the margarine in a 1-quart microwave-safe measuring cup. Microwave on High for 1 minute. Stir in the graham cracker crumbs and sugar. Pat the crumb mixture into a 9-inch microwave-safe pie plate. Microwave on High for 1 1/2 minutes. Let stand until cool.

Beat the egg substitute in a mixing bowl until frothy. Add the condensed milk and beat until blended. Stir in the lime juice. Pour into the prepared pie plate and bake in a preheated 350-degree oven for 10 minutes. Cool for 10 minutes and chill. Spread the whipped topping over the baked layer just before serving. You may freeze for future use. Low-fat sweetened condensed milk is not recommended for this recipe. If time is of the essence, use a commercially prepared graham cracker pie shell. *Yield: 6 servings.*

FLORIDA LIMES

Persian limes are the familiar market variety. They are relatively large and dark green in color. Select limes that are fresh, not leathery or shriveled at the stem end. A brownish circle at the pointed end can indicate rot or dryness.

Key limes are also called West Indian or Mexican limes. They are small, thin-skinned, and yellow-green in color. Famous as an ingredient in Key lime pie, they can also be used the same as limes or lemons. Bottled Key lime juice is available commercially in many supermarkets. Store both types of limes in the refrigerator at fifty-five degrees and use within one week.

MANGOES

No other fruit compares to the tropical flavor of a ripe mango, but the versatile fruit can be used at any stage of maturity. Each cultivar is slightly different in flavor and other characteristics from the others.

People who do not like mangoes may never have tasted a good, fully ripened fruit. Inferior varieties have a strong turpentine undertaste, which may explain why many visitors to South Florida have a poor impression of the mango upon first trying it. This is unfortunate as there is no resemblance between this fruit and the sweet, aromatic mangoes now being marketed.

Spicy Mango and Avocado Salsa

- 2 ripe avocados, chopped
- 2 ripe mangoes, chopped
- 1 small fully ripened fresh Florida red tomato, chopped
- 1 small fully ripened fresh Florida yellow tomato, chopped
- 1 small orange bell pepper, chopped
- 1 small red onion, chopped
- 1 bunch cilantro, trimmed and finely chopped
- Juice of 1 lime
- Juice of 2 tangerines, or 1 large orange
- Cayenne pepper (optional)
- Finely minced jalapeño chile (optional)

Combine the first seven ingredients in a nonreactive bowl and mix gently. Stir in the lime juice and tangerine juice. Season to taste with cayenne pepper and jalapeño chile. Chill, covered, for 1 hour. Serve with mild grilled fish or chicken. *Yield: 6 servings.*

Mango Cake

- 2 cups all-purpose flour
- 1 teaspoon baking powder
- 1 teaspoon baking soda
- 1/2 teaspoon salt
- 1 1/2 cups sugar
- 1/2 cup (1 stick) margarine
- 1 cup mashed mango
- 2 eggs
- 1/4 cup buttermilk
- 1 tablespoon vanilla extract
- 1 cup chopped pecans

Sift the flour, baking powder, baking soda and salt together. Beat the sugar and margarine in a mixing bowl until creamy, scraping the bowl occasionally. Beat in the mango and eggs. Blend in half the dry ingredients. Mix in the buttermilk and vanilla. Add the remaining ingredients and beat until combined.

Spoon the batter into a greased and floured 8×12-inch cake pan. Bake in a preheated 350 degree oven for 25 to 35 minutes or until the edges pull from the sides of the pan. Cool in the pan on a wire rack. *Yield: 9 servings.*

Crystallized Citrus Peel

2 cups fruit peel slices
2 gallons plus 1 1/3 cups water
2/3 cup corn syrup
1 1/3 cups sugar
1/2 teaspoon salt
1/2 cup sugar

Select bright fruit with thick peels. Strip the peel from the fruit in sections and cut enough of the peel into 1/4- to 1/2-inch strips to measure 2 cups. Combine 2 cups peel and 2 quarts of the water in a large saucepan. Bring to a simmer and simmer for 30 minutes, adding additional water if necessary. Drain and add 2 more quarts of the remaining water. Simmer for 30 minutes and drain. Repeat the process two more times with the remaining 2 quarts water; drain.

Combine the corn syrup, 1 1/3 cups sugar, the remaining 1 1/3 cups water and the salt in a saucepan and bring to a boil. Stir in the fruit peel and boil gently for 30 minutes. Reduce the heat to low and simmer for 30 to 40 minutes or until all of the syrup has been absorbed. Remove the peel and coat with 1/2 cup sugar. Arrange the crystallized peel in a single layer on a wire rack and let stand until cool. Store in airtight containers or freeze for future use. *Yield: 8 (1/4-cup) servings.*

Orange Juice Cake

1 (2-layer) package yellow
cake mix
1 (4-ounce) package lemon
instant pudding mix
4 eggs
3/4 cup corn oil
3/4 cup orange juice

Combine the cake mix, pudding mix, eggs, corn oil and orange juice in a mixing bowl. Beat at low speed for 2 minutes, scraping the bowl constantly. Spoon the batter into a greased and floured tube pan or 9×13-inch cake pan. Bake in preheated 325-degree oven for 45 minutes. *Yield: 10 servings.*

Orange Juice Cookies

1 (16-ounce) package vanilla wafers, crushed
1 (16-ounce) package confectioners' sugar
1 (6-ounce) can frozen orange juice concentrate, thawed
1/2 cup (1 stick) butter, softened
1 cup shredded coconut

Combine the vanilla wafer crumbs, confectioners' sugar, orange juice concentrate and butter in a bowl and mix well. Shape into small balls and coat with the coconut. Store in an airtight container in the refrigerator. *Yield: 36 cookies.*

Citrus Cookies

1 (16-ounce) package confectioners' sugar
1 (12-ounce) package vanilla wafers, crushed
1 (6-ounce) can frozen orange juice concentrate (do not thaw)
1/2 cup (1 stick) butter, softened
1 cup chopped pecans
1 cup confectioners' sugar

Combine the package of confectioners' sugar, vanilla wafer crumbs, orange juice concentrate, butter and pecans in a bowl and mix well. Shape into 1-inch balls and coat with 1 cup confectioners' sugar. Store in an airtight container in the refrigerator. You may alternatively coat the cookies with 1 cup chopped pecans. *Yield: 48 cookies.*

Papaya and Avocado Salad with Lime

1 papaya, cut into 1/2-inch pieces
1 avocado, cut into 1-inch pieces
1 (8-ounce) can sliced water chestnuts, drained
1 tomato, cut into 1/2-inch pieces
Juice from 1/2 lime
1 tablespoon Dijon mustard
1/2 small garlic clove, minced
Salt and freshly ground pepper to taste
1/3 cup olive oil
1 tablespoon balsamic vinegar

Combine the papaya, avocado, water chestnuts and tomato in a bowl and mix gently. Drizzle with the lime juice. Chill, covered, for 1 hour.

Whisk the Dijon mustard, garlic, salt and pepper in a small bowl until combined. Add the olive oil and vinegar gradually, whisking constantly until creamy. Adjust the seasonings to taste. Add to the papaya mixture and mix until coated. *Yield: 8 servings.*

Pineapple Mango Smoothie

4 ice cubes
1/2 cup frozen orange/strawberry/banana juice concentrate (do not thaw)
1/2 cup chopped fresh pineapple
1 cup chopped fresh mango
1 cup 1% milk
1 tablespoon honey

Process the ice cubes in a blender until crushed. Add the frozen juice concentrate, pineapple and mango and process until blended. Add the milk and honey and process until smooth. Pour into two glasses and serve immediately. *Yield: 2 servings.*

CAROTENOIDS IN TROPICAL FRUITS

Carotenoids are vitamin A precursors found in brightly colored fruits and vegetables. People who eat a diet rich in fruits and vegetables have reduced risk of chronic diseases, including stroke, Type 2 Diabetes, and some types of cancer.

Many tropical fruits are excellent sources of carotenoids. Mangoes are the richest source, with 805 Retinol Equivalents (RE) in one mango. Papaya has 85 RE, guava 71 RE, and carambola (star fruit) 62 RE in one fruit. One cup of fried ripe plantain contains 162 RE. The 2005 Dietary Guidelines recommends a daily intake of at least 1 1/2 cups of fruit. People who eat 2,000 to 2,800 calories per day should eat about 2 1/2 cups a day.

Escalloped Pineapple

2 (20-ounce) cans juice-pack pineapple tidbits
2 cups (8 ounces) shredded Cheddar cheese
1 cup sugar
6 tablespoons self-rising flour
1 sleeve butter crackers
1/2 cup (1 stick) butter, melted (do not use margarine)

Drain the pineapple, reserving the juice. Spread the pineapple in a 9×12-inch baking dish sprayed with nonstick cooking spray. Combine the cheese, sugar and self-rising flour in a sealable plastic bag and seal tightly. Shake to mix. Spread over the pineapple.

Crush the crackers in a sealable plastic bag. Add the butter to the cracker crumbs and shake to mix. Sprinkle the crumb mixture over the prepared layers and drizzle with 6 to 8 tablespoons of the reserved juice. Bake in a preheated 350-degree oven for 30 minutes. Cover with foil during the last few minutes of the baking process to prevent overbrowning if needed. *Yield: 12 servings.*

Black Raspberry Cobbler

4 cups fresh or frozen black raspberries
1 cup sugar
1 cup all-purpose flour
1 teaspoon baking powder
1/2 cup (1 stick) margarine, cut into pieces
1 cup milk

Spread the raspberries in a greased 8×11-inch baking pan and sprinkle with the sugar. Sift the flour and baking powder together and sprinkle over the prepared layers. Dot with the margarine and pour the milk over the top. Bake in a preheated 350-degree oven for 30 minutes. Serve warm with a dollop of vanilla ice cream. *Yield: 8 servings.*

Strawberry Angel Delight

1 (6-ounce) package strawberry gelatin
2 cups boiling water
2 cups sliced fresh strawberries
1 (15-ounce) angel food cake, torn into small pieces
2 cups vanilla ice cream, softened

Dissolve the gelatin in the boiling water in a heatproof bowl. Let stand until cool; do not chill. Alternate layers of the strawberries and angel food cake in a bundt pan until all the ingredients are used, beginning with the strawberries.

Stir the ice cream into the cooled gelatin mixture and pour over the prepared layers. Chill, covered, for 4 hours or longer. Loosen the edge of the congealed mixture with a thin knife. Dip the pan in hot water for 1 second and invert onto a serving plate. Slice and garnish each serving with a dollop of whipped topping.
Yield: 16 servings.

Frozen Strawberry Dessert

8 ounces cream cheese, softened
3/4 cup sugar
1 (20-ounce) can crushed pineapple, drained
1 (10-ounce) package frozen strawberries, thawed
2 bananas, sliced
1/2 cup chopped walnuts
12 ounces frozen whipped topping, thawed

Beat the cream cheese and sugar in a mixing bowl until creamy. Stir in the pineapple, strawberries, bananas and walnuts. Fold in the whipped topping. Spoon into an 8×8-inch dish and freeze, covered, until firm. Cut into squares and serve frozen.
Yield: 8 servings.

Caramelized Grilled Strawberries and Ice Cream

2 pints fresh strawberries, stems removed
2 tablespoons hazelnut oil
2 tablespoons walnut oil
2 tablespoons sugar
2 tablespoons coconut-flavored rum
1 pint vanilla ice cream
2 teaspoons balsamic vinegar

Toss the strawberries, hazelnut oil, walnut oil and sugar in a bowl until coated. Arrange the strawberries on an oiled grill rack and grill until black char marks appear on the strawberries, turning occasionally. Remove the strawberries to a bowl and coarsely chop. Add the rum to the strawberries and stir until combined.

Let stand, covered with plastic wrap, at room temperature for 2 hours. To serve, spoon 1/2 cup of the ice cream into each of four dessert bowls. Top with equal amounts of the strawberry mixture and drizzle each serving with 1/2 teaspoon of the vinegar. Garnish with sprigs of mint and serve immediately. *Yield: 4 servings.*

Strawberry Fruit Smoothie

1 cup strawberries
1 banana
1 cup vanilla nonfat yogurt
8 ice cubes
1 cup orange juice

Combine the strawberries, banana, yogurt and ice cubes in a blender. Add the orange juice gradually, processing constantly until of the desired consistency. Pour into two glasses and serve immediately. *Yield: 2 servings.*

Strawberry Pretzel Salad

2½ cups crushed pretzels
¾ cup (1½ sticks) margarine, softened
3 tablespoons brown sugar
1 (6-ounce) package strawberry gelatin
2 cups boiling water
2 (10-ounce) packages frozen strawberries, slightly thawed
8 ounces cream cheese, softened
1 cup granulated sugar
8 ounces whipped topping

Mix the pretzel crumbs, margarine and brown sugar in a bowl until combined. Press the crumb mixture over the bottom of a lightly buttered 9×13-inch baking pan. Bake in a preheated 350-degree oven for 10 minutes. Let stand until cool.

Dissolve the gelatin in the boiling water in a heatproof bowl. Add the chilled strawberries to the hot gelatin and mix well. Cool until the gelatin mixture begins to set.

Beat the cream cheese, granulated sugar and whipped topping in a mixing bowl until creamy. Spread the cream cheese mixture over the crumb mixture and top with the gelatin mixture. Chill, covered, until set. *Yield: 16 servings.*

STRAWBERRIES

The strawberry, a member of the rose family, is unique in that it is the only fruit with seeds on the outside rather than the inside.

The wide distribution of wild strawberries is largely from the seeds sown by birds. It seems that when birds eat the wild berries the seeds pass through them intact and in reasonably good condition. The germinating seeds respond to light rather than moisture and therefore need no covering of earth to start growing.

The Native Americans were already eating strawberries when the colonists arrived. The crushed berries were mixed with cornmeal and baked into strawberry bread. After trying this bread, the colonists developed their own version of the recipe and thus Strawberry Shortcake was created.

Roasted Strawberry and Tomato Soup

2 pints fresh strawberries, stems removed
1 pint cherry tomatoes
1/4 cup chopped fresh fennel
1/4 cup olive oil
1 cup bottled strawberry daiquiri mix
Salt and pepper to taste

Toss the strawberries, tomatoes, fennel and olive oil in a bowl until coated. Spread in a single layer on a baking sheet and roast in a preheated 350-degree oven for 15 minutes.

Process the roasted strawberry mixture in a blender until puréed. Add the daiquiri mix and process until blended. Strain the soup through a fine mesh strainer into a bowl. Season to taste with salt and pepper and chill until serving time. Ladle into soup bowls. *Yield: 4 servings.*

Depression Cracker Pie

3 egg whites
1/2 teaspoon cream of tartar
1 cup sugar
1 teaspoon vanilla extract
18 saltine crackers, crushed
1 cup pecans, chopped
8 ounces frozen whipped topping, thawed
3 cups frozen sliced sweetened strawberries, thawed and drained

Beat the egg whites in a mixing bowl until foamy. Add the cream of tartar and beat until stiff peaks form. Add the sugar and vanilla gradually, beating constantly until blended. Fold in the cracker crumbs and pecans.

Spread in a buttered 9-inch pie plate. Bake in a preheated 325-degree oven for 30 minutes. Cool on a wire rack. Mix the whipped topping and strawberries in a bowl and spread over the baked layer. Chill until serving time. *Yield: 8 servings.*

Vanilla-Grilled Lobster with Florida Strawberry, Fennel and Pistachio Salad and Tangerine Butter

Grilled Lobster
2 vanilla beans, split and scraped
1/2 cup plus 2 tablespoons canola oil
4 (4-ounce) lobster tails, split
Salt and pepper to taste

Strawberry, Fennel and Pistachio Salad
2 pints fresh strawberries, cut into halves
1 fennel bulb, thinly sliced
1 red onion, thinly sliced
1 tablespoon minced fennel leaves
1/2 cup pistachios, roasted and chopped
Sections of 1 tangerine, cut into thirds
Juice of 1 tangerine
Salt and pepper to taste

Tangerine Butter
Juice of 4 tangerines
1/4 cup white wine
1 shallot, minced
3 to 8 peppercorns
1 bay leaf
2 tablespoons heavy cream
1/4 cup (1/2 stick) butter, cut into pieces
Salt and pepper to taste

To prepare the lobster, combine the vanilla seeds and canola oil in a bowl. Reserve 2 tablespoons of the vanilla oil for the salad. Pour the remaining vanilla oil over the lobster in a shallow dish. Marinate in the refrigerator for 30 to 60 minutes. Season with salt and pepper and grill until cooked through.

To prepare the salad, combine the reserved 2 tablespoons vanilla oil, strawberries, sliced fennel, onion, fennel fronds, pistachios, tangerine and tangerine juice in a bowl and mix gently. Season with salt and pepper.

To prepare the butter, combine the tangerine juice, wine, shallot, peppercorns and bay leaf in a small saucepan and bring to a boil. Reduce the heat to low and simmer until the mixture is reduced to a syrupy consistency, stirring occasionally. Add the heavy cream and simmer for 1 minute. Remove from the heat. Add the butter one piece at a time, whisking until combined after each addition. Season to taste with salt and pepper. Strain into a bowl, discarding the solids.

To serve, drizzle equal amounts of the butter onto four serving plates. Mound one-fourth of the salad on each prepared plate and top each with a grilled lobster tail. Serve immediately. *Yield: 4 servings.*

Watermelon Granita-Filled Lime Cups

12 limes
2 cups water
1 cup sugar
4 cups cubed watermelon
1/2 cup dark raisins
Crushed ice (optional)

Cut the limes lengthwise into halves. Cut around the pulp of each half with a sharp knife, leaving the peel intact. Scoop out the pulp, using a spoon to loosen the pulp from the peel. Reserve 2 tablespoons of the lime juice and discard the pulp.

Bring the water and sugar to a boil in a small saucepan. Remove from the heat and let stand until cool. Pulse the watermelon in a food processor until puréed. Place a colander over a bowl. Pour the purée into the colander to strain out the seeds, forcing the watermelon through the colander with the back of a spoon if needed. Stir the reserved lime juice and cooled sugar mixture into the watermelon purée. Pour the watermelon mixture into a 9×13-inch dish and freeze for 4 hours or until firm.

To serve, scrape the frozen watermelon mixture with a spoon into a bowl and stir in the raisins for "seeds." Mound the granita in the lime cups and serve on a bed of crushed ice. *Yield: 24 (1-lime cup) servings.*

Watermelon Lemonade

6 cups cubed seeded watermelon
1 cup water
1/4 cup raspberries
1/3 cup sugar, or an equivalent amount of sugar substitute
1/2 cup lemon juice

Combine the watermelon, water and raspberries in a blender and process until smooth. Strain the watermelon mixture through a fine mesh strainer into a pitcher, discarding the solids. Add the sugar and lemon juice and stir until the sugar dissolves. Chill for 1 hour or longer. *Yield: 4 servings.*

Watermelon and Spinach Salad

Salad
6 cups torn fresh spinach
3 cups cubed seeded watermelon
1 cup sliced fresh mushrooms
1 slice turkey bacon, crisp-cooked and crumbled

Balsamic Vinaigrette
1/3 cup balsamic or red wine vinegar
1/4 cup sugar
1/4 cup chopped onion
1 teaspoon Worcestershire sauce
3 tablespoons vegetable oil
1/2 teaspoon salt

To prepare the salad, toss the spinach, watermelon, mushrooms and bacon in a bowl until combined.

To prepare the vinaigrette, combine the vinegar, sugar, onion, Worcestershire sauce, oil and salt in a blender or food processor and process until blended. Just before serving toss the salad with 1/3 cup of the vinaigrette. *Yield: 6 servings.*

The nutritional profile contains 1/3 cup of the vinaigrette.

Fruited Ice

1 cup sugar
1 cup water
1 (20-ounce) can crushed pineapple
1 (16-ounce) can apricot halves, drained and chopped
1 quart fresh strawberries, chopped, or 1 (16-ounce) package frozen strawberries, chopped and drained
2 bananas, chopped

Bring the sugar and water to a boil in a 2-quart saucepan and remove from the heat. Add the undrained pineapple, apricots and strawberries and mix well. Stir in the bananas.

Fill thirty foil baking cups with the fruit mixture and freeze until firm. Unmold and arrange on lettuce-lined or spinach-lined salad plates. *Yield: 30 servings.*

STAR FRUIT OF FLORIDA

Carambola is the star-shaped fruit of Florida. The fruit was introduced to Florida nearly one hundred years ago and they are best eaten when the fruit is a mixture of yellow and green on the outside. They are usually cut crosswise to reveal the star-shape and added raw to salads and fruit cups. Carambola are also used as a garnish for cooked poultry, seafood, and meats.

Many say the flavor is a mix of apples, grapes, and citrus all in one bite. Star fruit are high in vitamin C, but are usually not consumed in large quantities.

Tropical Fruit Mold

1 papaya
1 mango
1 carambola (star fruit)
1 cup strawberries, sliced
1 1/4 cups orange juice
1 envelope unflavored gelatin
2 tablespoons Chambord or orange liqueur
1 mango
1/2 cup orange juice

Cut the papaya into halves. Seed, peel and cut one half into 1/2-inch pieces. Cut the remaining half into slices and reserve. Cut 1 mango on either side of the seed. Scoop out the pulp and cut into 1/2-inch pieces. Cut the carambola into 1/2-inch pieces or stars. Combine the papaya, mango, carambola and strawberries in a 5×9-inch loaf pan.

Pour 2/3 cup of the orange juice into a small saucepan and sprinkle with the gelatin. Let stand for 5 minutes. Cook over low heat until the gelatin dissolves, stirring occasionally. Let stand until cool and stir in the remaining orange juice. Add the liqueur and mix well. Pour over the fruit mixture and chill for 4 hours or until set.

Cut 1 mango on either side of the seed. Reserve a few slices of the mango for decoration. Scoop out the mango pulp and place in a blender or food processor fitted with a steel blade. Reserve several slices of the reserved sliced papaya. Add the remaining papaya and 1/2 cup orange juice to the blender and process until puréed.

To serve, dip the loaf pan in hot water and invert the fruit mold onto a serving plate. Cut into eight slices. Drizzle each slice with some of the papaya purée on dessert plates. Top with the reserved papaya slices and reserved mango slices. *Yield: 8 servings.*

Farm-Fresh Vegetables

Farm-Fresh Vegetables

Herbed Green Beans

- 1 pound fresh green beans, cut into 2-inch pieces
- 2 tablespoons water
- 1/2 cup chopped onion
- 1/4 cup finely chopped celery
- 1 to 3 tablespoons butter or margarine
- 1 garlic clove, minced
- 1/2 teaspoon dried rosemary, crushed
- 1/2 teaspoon dried basil

Combine the green beans and water in a 2-quart microwave-safe dish. Microwave, covered, on High for 4 to 6 minutes or until tender; drain. Combine the onion, celery, butter, garlic, rosemary and basil in a microwave-safe dish. Microwave, covered, on High for 2 minutes or until the onion is tender. Add the onion mixture to the green beans and toss to combine. *Yield: 6 servings.*

Broccoli Salad

- 1 head broccoli, trimmed and cut into bite-size pieces
- 1 tablespoon water
- 1 head lettuce, chopped
- 6 hard-cooked eggs, sliced
- 1 purple onion, sliced
- 1 cup mayonnaise
- 3 tablespoons red wine vinegar
- 1 teaspoon sugar
- Pepper to taste

Combine the broccoli and water in a microwave-safe dish. Microwave, covered, for 1 to 2 minutes or until tender-crisp. Let stand until cool. Mix the broccoli, lettuce, eggs and onion in a bowl.

Combine the mayonnaise, vinegar, sugar and pepper in a bowl and mix well. Add to the broccoli mixture, stirring gently until coated. Chill, covered, until serving time. *Yield: 10 servings.*

USING HERBS

When using herbs in cooking, also chop and use the soft stems of some herbs such as parsley and cilantro. The stem portions can be measured along with the leaves. Some stems are too woody to use, such as thyme and rosemary. Thick, woody stems can be used as skewers for grilling meats and vegetables.

Celery leaves can also be used. They can be added to salads and soups. Just rinse, chop, and combine with the other ingredients. Remember when using dried herbs that only one-third of the amount of fresh is required.

Broccoli Raisin Salad

- 1 head broccoli, trimmed and cut into bite-size pieces
- 1/4 cup finely chopped onion
- 1/4 cup raisins
- 1 cup mayonnaise-type salad dressing or mayonnaise
- 1/4 cup sugar
- 2 tablespoons vinegar
- 1/4 cup chopped pecans
- 4 slices bacon, crisp-cooked and crumbled

Mix the broccoli, onion and raisins in a bowl. Combine the salad dressing, sugar and vinegar in a bowl and mix well. Add to the broccoli mixture and toss until coated. Chill, covered, in the refrigerator.

Stir in the pecans and bacon just before serving. For variety, add shredded sharp Cheddar cheese. You may alternatively use turkey bacon. *Yield: 8 servings.*

Light Cream of Broccoli Soup

- 1 (16-ounce) package low-sodium fat-free chicken broth
- 1/3 cup nonfat dry milk powder
- 3 tablespoons cornstarch
- 1/2 teaspoon dried onion flakes
- 1/4 teaspoon salt
- 1/4 teaspoon dried basil
- 1/4 teaspoon dried thyme
- 1/4 teaspoon pepper
- 1 (10-ounce) package frozen chopped broccoli, thawed and drained
- 1 1/2 cups fat-free milk
- 1/3 cup shredded reduced-fat Cheddar cheese
- 1 tablespoon butter-flavor granules

Combine the broth, milk powder, cornstarch, onion flakes, salt, basil, thyme and pepper in a large saucepan and mix well. Bring to a boil. Boil for 1 minute, stirring constantly.

Add the broccoli, milk, cheese and butter-flavor granules to the broth mixture and mix well. Cook until the cheese melts and the soup is heated through, stirring occasionally. Ladle into soup bowls. Garnish each serving with 1/2 teaspoon shredded reduced-fat Cheddar cheese, if desired. *Yield: 4 servings.*

Broccoslaw

1 (12-ounce) package broccoli slaw
1 cup sunflower seeds
1/2 to 1 cup slivered almonds
4 scallions, chopped, or 1/2 cup chopped sweet onion
1/3 cup canola oil
1/3 cup white vinegar
1/3 cup sugar, or an equivalent amount of sugar substitute
2 packages ramen noodles, crushed (discard flavor packets)

Combine the slaw, sunflower seeds, almonds and scallions in a bowl and mix well. Whisk the canola oil, vinegar and sugar in a bowl until the sugar dissolves. Pour over the slaw mixture and toss until coated. Add the noodles and mix well. Chill, covered, for 2 to 10 hours. *Yield: 8 servings.*

Blue Ribbon Coleslaw

2 cups shredded green cabbage
2 cups shredded red cabbage
1/4 to 1/2 cup shredded carrots
1/2 to 3/4 cup mayonnaise or light mayonnaise
2 tablespoons cider vinegar
2 tablespoons milk
1/2 cup dried cranberries
1 1/2 teaspoons ground celery seeds
1/2 teaspoon sugar

Toss the cabbage and carrots in a bowl. Whisk the mayonnaise, vinegar and milk in a bowl until smooth. Fold into the cabbage mixture. Add the cranberries, celery seeds and sugar and stir until combined. Chill, covered, for 2 hours. *Yield: 8 servings.*

Florida Coleslaw

2 cups fat-free sour cream
1 envelope onion soup mix
2 quarts shredded cabbage
4 carrots, coarsely grated
1 green bell pepper, chopped
4 teaspoons cider vinegar

Combine the sour cream and soup mix in a large bowl and mix well. Add the cabbage, carrots, bell pepper and vinegar and mix well. Chill, covered, in the refrigerator. For variety, substitute a mixture of 1/4 cup bottled blue cheese salad dressing and 1/4 cup reduced-calorie mayonnaise for 1 cup of the sour cream. *Yield: 8 servings.*

Frozen Coleslaw

1 (3-pound) head cabbage, shredded
1 teaspoon salt
2 cups sugar, or equivalent amount of sugar substitute
1 cup vinegar
1 teaspoon celery seeds
1 teaspoon mustard seeds
1 carrot, shredded
1 bell pepper, minced

Toss the cabbage with the salt in a bowl. Let stand for 1 hour. Press the excess moisture from the cabbage. Mix the sugar, vinegar, celery seeds and mustard seeds in a saucepan and bring to a boil.

Boil for 1 minute. Remove from the heat and let stand until cool. Pour the vinegar mixture over the cabbage and mix well. Freeze, covered, in the freezer. Add the carrot and bell pepper after the slaw has been frozen and thawed. You may also serve fresh. *Yield: 8 servings.*

Copper Pennies

- 2 pounds carrots, sliced
- 1 (10-ounce) can tomato soup
- 1 cup sugar
- 3/4 cup vinegar
- 1/2 cup vegetable oil
- 1 teaspoon Worcestershire sauce
- 1 teaspoon dry mustard
- Salt and pepper to taste
- 1 bell pepper, cut into rings
- 1 onion, sliced and separated into rings

Combine the carrots with enough water to cover in a saucepan. Cook until tender-crisp; drain. Rinse the carrots with cold water and drain.

Heat the soup, sugar, vinegar, oil, Worcestershire sauce, dry mustard, salt and pepper in a saucepan until blended, stirring occasionally. Layer the carrots, bell pepper and onion in a shallow dish. Pour the tomato soup mixture over the prepared layers and chill, covered, in the refrigerator. *Yield: 8 servings.*

Garden Waldorf Salad

- 3 cups broccoli florets
- 1 1/2 cups sliced cauliflower
- 1 cup grated carrots
- 1 cup chopped apples
- 1/2 cup chopped green onions
- 1/4 cup chopped peanuts
- 1 cup vanilla nonfat yogurt

Toss the broccoli, cauliflower, carrots, apples, green onions and peanuts in a bowl. Add the yogurt and stir until coated. Chill, covered, in the refrigerator for up to 6 hours. *Yield: 4 servings.*

FLAVORED VINEGARS

Any of Florida's fruits can be combined with apple cider vinegar or Champagne vinegar to create a flavored vinegar. Start with a clean, sterilized jar or container with a tight-fitting lid. (Sterilize by covering jars with water and boiling for 10 minutes.) Add your favorite fruit, herbs, and/or spices. Use 3 to 4 sprigs of fresh herbs, 3 tablespoons dried herbs, or 1 to 2 cups of fruit. Herbs and berries can be "lightly bruised" as they are added to the jars to heighten the infusion of flavors. Heat the vinegar to 190 to 195 degrees and pour into the jars, leaving a 1/4-inch headspace. Seal with tight-fitting lids and store in a cool, dark environment for 3 to 4 weeks to allow the flavors to develop. Use with salads, vegetables, and meats.

Cauliflower Salad

Creamy Blue Cheese Dressing
1 cup reduced-fat mayonnaise
1 cup reduced-fat or fat-free sour cream
4 ounces blue cheese, crumbled
1 envelope ranch salad dressing mix
2 teaspoons caraway seeds

Salad
1 head cauliflower, chopped into small florets
1 cup sliced radishes
1 cup chopped green onions
1 (4-ounce) can sliced water chestnuts, drained

To prepare the dressing, mix the mayonnaise, sour cream, blue cheese, salad dressing mix and caraway seeds in a bowl. Chill, covered, for 1 to 10 hours.

To prepare the salad, toss the cauliflower, radishes, green onions and water chestnuts in a bowl. Add the dressing and stir until coated. Chill for one hour or longer before serving. *Yield: 6 servings.*

Cucumber Salad

1 (3-ounce) package lime gelatin
1 cup boiling water
1 cup sour cream
1 cucumber, shredded
1 teaspoon grated onion

Dissolve the gelatin in the boiling water in a heatproof bowl. Chill until partially set. Stir in the sour cream, cucumber and onion and spoon the gelatin mixture into an 8×8-inch dish. Chill until firm. *Yield: 6 servings.*

Eggplant Casserole

5 slices bacon
1 onion, chopped
1 eggplant, peeled and chopped
3 large fully ripened fresh Florida tomatoes, chopped
1 teaspoon sugar
1/2 teaspoon salt
1/2 teaspoon pepper
2 tablespoons finely chopped fresh parsley
1 teaspoon dried basil leaves, crushed
1 cup (4 ounces) shredded Cheddar cheese

Cook the bacon in a skillet until brown and crisp. Remove the bacon to a paper towel to drain, reserving the pan drippings. Crumble the bacon. Sauté the onion in the reserved pan drippings until tender. Stir in the eggplant, tomatoes, sugar, salt and pepper. Simmer, covered, for 10 minutes, stirring occasionally. Add the bacon, parsley and basil and mix well.

Spoon into a lightly greased 1-quart baking dish and sprinkle with the cheese. Bake in a preheated 350-degree oven for 10 minutes or until the cheese melts. *Yield: 6 servings.*

Spring Peas

1/4 to 1/2 head lettuce
1 tablespoon margarine, melted
2 (10-ounce) packages frozen peas, thawed
1 tablespoon sugar
1 teaspoon seasoned salt
1 tablespoon imitation bacon bits

Cut the lettuce into thin slices, approximately 1 inch in length; do not shred. Drizzle the margarine over the bottom of an 8×8-inch dish, tilting the dish to ensure even coverage. Cover the margarine with half of the lettuce. Spread one package of the peas over the lettuce. Sprinkle with 1 1/2 teaspoons of the sugar and 1/2 teaspoon of the salt. Layer with the remaining lettuce, remaining package of peas, remaining 1 1/2 teaspoons sugar and remaining 1/2 teaspoon salt. Top with the bacon bits. *Yield: 6 servings.*

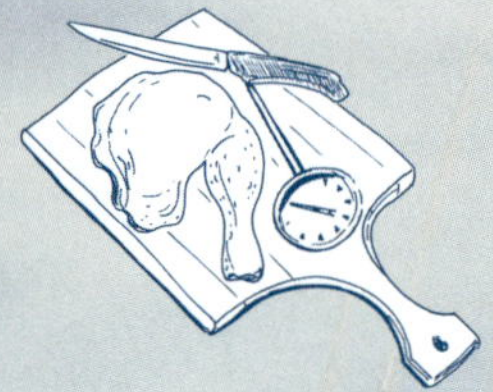

STORAGE AND USE OF POTATOES

Store potatoes in a cool, dark, and dry environment. Do not rinse before storing, and do not place them in the refrigerator, as this imparts an undesirable taste as their starch turns to sugar. Potatoes can be stored in brown, perforated plastic, or burlap bags.

When stored properly at home, potatoes can be kept for up to two months. Do not store them with onions, as they give off a natural gas that quickens the decaying of the potatoes and vice versa. Storing with an apple will help keep the potatoes from sprouting. If your potatoes have sprouted, they can still be used. Just break off the sprouts and use the potatoes in your favorite way.

Hot Potato Salad

- 5 pounds unpeeled potatoes, chopped
- 1 1/2 cups mayonnaise or reduced-fat mayonnaise
- 1 1/2 cups chopped onions
- 1/2 cup sweet pickle relish
- 4 to 6 hard-cooked eggs, chopped
- Salt and pepper to taste

Combine the potatoes with enough water to cover in a large saucepan and bring to a boil. Boil for 30 minutes or until tender; drain in a colander.

Combine the mayonnaise, onions, pickle relish and eggs in a bowl and mix well. Layer the potatoes and mayonnaise mixture one-half at a time in a large salad bowl and toss lightly. Season to taste with salt and pepper. Serve warm or chilled. For enhanced flavor, hard-cook the eggs immediately before adding to the salad. *Yield: 20 servings.*

Hungarian Potato Salad

- 2 large potatoes, peeled, cut into small chunks and cooked
- 1 carrot, chopped and cooked
- 4 ounces cauliflower florets, cooked until tender-crisp
- 1/2 cup fresh or frozen green peas, cooked
- 1/4 cup light mayonnaise
- 1 to 2 teaspoons lemon juice
- Salt and pepper to taste
- 1 hard-cooked egg, chopped
- 2 black olives, minced

Mix the potatoes, carrot, cauliflower and peas in a large bowl. Combine the mayonnaise, lemon juice, salt and pepper in a bowl and mix well. Stir in the egg and olives. Add to the potato mixture and mix gently until coated. Chill, covered, in the refrigerator until serving time. *Yield: 4 servings.*

Make-Ahead Mashed Potatoes

3 pounds potatoes, peeled and chopped
6 ounces Neufchâtel cheese, softened
1 cup light sour cream
1/4 cup low-fat milk
2 tablespoons margarine
1/2 teaspoon salt (optional)
Margarine (optional)
1/2 teaspoon paprika (optional)

Combine the potatoes with enough water to cover in a saucepan and bring to a boil. Boil until tender; drain. Mash the potatoes in a bowl. Add the cheese, sour cream, milk, 2 tablespoons margarine and the salt and stir until blended.

Spoon into an 8×12-inch baking dish. Dot with additional margarine and sprinkle with paprika. Chill or freeze, covered, for future use. Just before serving thaw in the refrigerator if frozen and bake in a preheated 350-degree oven for 30 to 45 minutes or until heated through and brown on top. You may freeze in smaller baking dishes. *Yield: 8 servings.*

Party Potatoes

1 (2-pound) package frozen hash brown potatoes
2 (10-ounce) cans cream of mushroom soup
2 cups sour cream
8 ounces Cheddar cheese, shredded
1 cup chopped onion
6 tablespoons butter, melted
1 teaspoon salt
1/2 teaspoon garlic salt
2 cups cornflakes, crushed
3/4 cup (1 1/2 sticks) margarine, melted

Combine the potatoes, soup, sour cream, cheese, onion, 6 tablespoons butter, the salt and garlic salt in a bowl and mix well. Spoon the potato mixture into a 9×13-inch baking pan.

Toss the cornflake crumbs and 3/4 cup margarine in a bowl until coated and sprinkle over the prepared layer. Bake in a preheated 350-degree oven for 1 1/4 hours. *Yield: 12 servings.*

FLORIDA'S NEW LOW-CARB POTATO

*Consumers are going to love the flavor and appearance of **SunLite Gold** potatoes, and the fact that they have 30 percent fewer carbohydrates than a standard russet baking potato. This new potato does not look or taste like anything that's now on the market and it is not a genetically engineered crop. It has a smooth, buff-colored skin and light yellow flesh. Three and one-half ounces of the potato contains about 13 grams of carbohydrate compared to around 19 grams in the same size serving of a russet Burbank potato.*

USE CAUTION WHEN HANDLING HOT CHILES

Wear rubber or plastic gloves when handling hot chiles. Wash hands thoroughly with soap and water before touching the face or eyes. If your bare hands come in contact with hot chiles and a burning sensation persists, soak hands in a bowl of milk.

If someone has consumed chiles that were too hot or spicy, encourage them to drink milk, rinsing the mouth as they swallow. Yogurt or ice cream will also aid in cooling the "fire." Other options include eating rice or bread which will absorb the capsaicin, drinking tomato juice, or eating a fresh lemon or lime. Water does not mix with the oil base of capsaicin and will only distribute it to more parts of the mouth.

Hot and Spicy Potato Soup

2 slices turkey bacon
1 cup chopped onion
$^1/_2$ cup chopped poblano chiles
2 tablespoons minced seeded jalapeño chile
3 garlic cloves, minced
$^1/_2$ teaspoon ground cumin
2 (16-ounce) cans fat-free chicken broth
5 cups chopped peeled baking potatoes
$^1/_2$ teaspoon salt
2$^1/_2$ cups fat-free milk
$^1/_3$ cup all-purpose flour
5 ounces reduced-fat jalapeño Cheddar cheese, shredded
2 ounces reduced-fat Cheddar cheese, shredded
$^2/_3$ cup chopped green onions

Cook the bacon in a large saucepan until brown and crisp. Drain, reserving 1 tablespoon of the pan drippings. Crumble the bacon.

Sauté the onion, poblano chiles, jalapeño chile, garlic and cumin in the reserved pan drippings until golden brown. Stir in the broth, potatoes and salt and bring to a boil. Reduce the heat to low and simmer, covered, for 25 minutes or until the potatoes are tender.

Whisk the milk and flour in a bowl until blended. Gradually add to the potato mixture, stirring constantly. Cook over medium heat for 12 to 15 minutes or until thickened, stirring occasionally. Remove from the heat and add the cheeses, stirring until melted. Ladle into soup bowls and sprinkle with equal amounts of the green onions and bacon. *Yield: 10 (1-cup) servings.*

Whipped Rutabagas au Gratin

- 3 pounds rutabagas, cooked and mashed
- 1/4 cup (1/2 stick) margarine, melted
- 3 eggs
- 1 tablespoon sugar
- 1 cup bread crumbs
- 2 tablespoons margarine, melted

Beat the rutabagas, 1/4 cup margarine, the eggs and sugar in a mixing bowl until smooth and light. Spoon into a greased 3-quart baking dish. Sprinkle with the bread crumbs and drizzle with 2 tablespoons margarine. Bake in a preheated 350-degree oven for 50 to 60 minutes or until light brown. *Yield: 6 servings.*

NOTE: Rutabagas are hard to cut. Place the rutabaga on top of a paper towel. Make small slices through the shell. Microwave on High for 5 to 10 minutes and let stand until cool. The shell should be soft enough to easily slice and remove.

Egg and Spinach Salad

- 1 pound fresh spinach, trimmed
- 1/2 cup vegetable oil
- 1/4 cup sugar
- 2 tablespoons vinegar
- 1 teaspoon finely grated onion
- 1/2 teaspoon salt
- 1/4 teaspoon dry mustard
- 6 slices bacon, crisp-cooked, drained and crumbled
- 6 hard-cooked eggs, chopped

Rinse the spinach in lukewarm water and drain. Chill to crisp. Whisk the oil, sugar, vinegar, onion, salt and dry mustard in a mixing bowl until the sugar dissolves and the dressing is of a thick, syrupy consistency.

Tear the spinach into bite-size pieces and place in a large salad bowl. Add the bacon and eggs. Pour the dressing over the spinach mixture and let stand for 30 minutes. Toss to combine. Process the dressing in a blender, if desired. *Yield: 6 servings.*

NOTE: For convenience, prepare the dressing in advance and store in the refrigerator.

Spinach Pie

- 3/4 cup olive oil
- 1 (10-ounce) package frozen spinach, thawed and drained
- 1/2 cup chopped onion
- 1 teaspoon salt
- 1/2 cup milk
- 2 eggs
- 1/2 (1-pound) package phyllo
- 8 ounces crumbled feta cheese

Coat an 8×14-inch baking pan with 2 tablespoons of the olive oil. Heat 2 tablespoons of the olive oil in a sauté pan. Add the spinach, onion and salt and cook until the onion is tender. Whisk the remaining 1/2 cup olive oil, the milk and eggs in a bowl until blended. Arrange two sheets of the phyllo over the bottom of the prepared pan and brush with the egg mixture. Continue layering the phyllo two sheets at a time in the pan until half the phyllo has been used, brushing the sheets with the egg mixture. Spread with the spinach mixture and sprinkle with the cheese. Top with the remaining phyllo, two sheets at a time, brushing each layer with the egg mixture. Bake in a preheated 350-degree oven for 35 minutes. Cool and cut into squares. *Yield: 4 servings.*

Squash Casserole

- 1 pound yellow squash, sliced
- 1 pound zucchini, sliced
- 1 pound carrots, shredded
- 1 onion, finely chopped
- 1/4 cup water
- 1 teaspoon each salt and pepper
- 1 (8-ounce) package herb-seasoned stuffing mix
- 1 (10-ounce) can cream of chicken soup
- 1 cup light sour cream
- 1/2 cup 2% milk
- 1/2 cup (1 stick) butter or margarine, melted
- 1/2 cup (2 ounces) shredded Cheddar cheese

Combine the vegetables and water in a 4-quart microwave-safe dish. Microwave for 4 to 8 minutes or until the vegetables are tender; drain. Season with the salt and pepper. Reserve 1 cup of the stuffing mix. Mix the remaining stuffing mix with the remaining ingredients in a bowl. Stir into the vegetable mixture. Sprinkle with the 1 cup reserved stuffing mix and bake in a preheated 350-degree oven for 30 to 40 minutes or until brown and bubbly. *Yield: 16 servings.*

Acorn Squash Soufflé

- 1/2 cup (1 stick) butter or margarine
- 2 tablespoons all-purpose flour
- 1 cup milk
- 1 teaspoon chopped onion
- 1 1/2 teaspoons salt
- 1/8 teaspoon pepper
- 2 egg yolks, lightly beaten
- 2 cups shredded carrots
- 2 cups cooked acorn squash
- 3/4 cup cracker crumbs
- 1 cup (4 ounces) shredded Cheddar cheese
- 2 egg whites

Melt the butter in a heavy saucepan over low heat. Add the flour and cook until thickened and bubbly, stirring constantly. Stir in the milk gradually. Cook until smooth and thickened, stirring constantly. Stir in the onion, salt and pepper. Remove from the heat and cool slightly. Add the egg yolks and beat until blended. Stir in the carrots, squash, cracker crumbs and cheese.

Beat the egg whites in a bowl until stiff but not dry peaks form. Fold into the squash mixture. Spoon into a greased baking dish or soufflé dish. Bake in a preheated 350-degree oven for 45 minutes or until a knife inserted in the center comes out clean. *Yield: 8 servings.*

HERB SHAKERS FOR VEGETABLES

The following recipes are great alternatives to salt and can be used to spice up vegetables, salads, meat, and poultry.

*For **All-Around Mix**, combine 2 teaspoons garlic powder, 2 teaspoons onion powder, 2 teaspoons paprika, 2 teaspoons white pepper, 2 teaspoons dry mustard, 1 teaspoon ground thyme and 1 teaspoon ground celery seeds in a bowl and pour into a shaker.*

*For **Peppy Mix**, combine 1 1/2 tablespoons thyme leaves, 1 1/2 tablespoons marjoram leaves, 1 tablespoon rosemary leaves, 2 teaspoons ground sage and 1 teaspoon ground pepper in a blender. Process on high for 1 minute or until of a powdery consistency. Store in a shaker.*

Zucchini Relish

10 cups minced unpeeled zucchini
2 cups minced green bell pepper
4 cups minced onions
1 cup minced red bell pepper
5 tablespoons canning salt
4 1/2 cups sugar
2 1/2 cups white vinegar
2 tablespoons celery seeds
2 tablespoons cornstarch
1 tablespoon dry mustard
1 tablespoon pepper
1 tablespoon ground nutmeg
1 teaspoon turmeric

Combine the zucchini, green bell pepper, onions and red bell pepper in a bowl or crock. Sprinkle with the canning salt and let stand at room temperature for 8 to 10 hours. Drain and rinse with cold water; drain.

Mix the sugar, vinegar, celery seeds, cornstarch, dry mustard, pepper, nutmeg and turmeric in a stockpot and bring to a boil. Stir in the zucchini mixture and reduce the heat. Simmer for 30 minutes.

Spoon the relish into six hot sterilized pint jars, leaving a 1/2 inch headspace. Wipe the jar rims and seal with two-piece lids. Process in a boiling water bath for 10 minutes.
Yield: 192 (1-tablespoon) servings.

NOTE: This is delicious in chicken salad or potato salad. For additional directions on food preservation, call your county UF/IFAS Extension office or www.solutionsforyourlife.com.

Zucchini Soufflé

- 4 to 5 cups grated zucchini (6 zucchini or 1 1/2 pounds zucchini)
- 1 tablespoon salt
- 1/4 cup baking mix
- 4 eggs, lightly beaten
- 1/4 cup chopped fresh parsley or green bell pepper
- Salt and pepper to taste
- Garlic salt to taste
- 1 cup (4 ounces) shredded Cheddar cheese
- Sliced black olives or crumbled bacon (optional)

Mix the zucchini and salt in a bowl and let stand for 30 minutes. Remove to a colander and drain thoroughly.

Combine the baking mix, eggs, parsley, salt, pepper and garlic salt in a bowl and mix well. Add the zucchini and cheese and stir until combined. Spoon into a greased 2-quart baking dish and sprinkle with olives or bacon. Bake in a preheated 375-degree oven for 30 minutes or until set. Serve immediately. *Yield: 6 servings.*

Zucchini and Carrot Spice Muffins

- 2 cups all-purpose flour
- 1 1/4 cups packed brown sugar
- 2 teaspoons baking soda
- 1 1/2 teaspoons ground cinnamon
- 1/2 teaspoon ground allspice
- 1/2 teaspoon ground nutmeg
- 1/2 teaspoon salt
- 1 cup vegetable oil
- 3 eggs
- 1/2 teaspoon vanilla extract
- 1 1/2 cups grated zucchini
- 1 1/2 cups grated carrots
- 1/2 cup chopped pecans

Sift the flour, brown sugar, baking soda, cinnamon, allspice, nutmeg and salt into a large bowl and mix well. Whisk the oil, eggs and vanilla in a bowl until blended. Stir in the zucchini and carrots. Add to the flour mixture and stir just until moistened. Fold in the pecans.

Spoon the batter into greased muffin cups. Bake in a preheated 375-degree oven for 18 to 20 minutes or until a wooden pick inserted in the centers comes out clean. Cool in the pan for 2 minutes and remove to a wire rack. *Yield: 24 muffins.*

Zucchini with Walnuts

1 1/2 tablespoons olive oil
1 tablespoon margarine or butter
6 zucchini, cut into 1/4-inch slices
1 unpeeled garlic clove
1/2 cup coarsely chopped walnuts
Salt and pepper to taste

Heat the olive oil and margarine in a medium skillet until the margarine melts. Add the zucchini and sauté until tender but slightly firm, shaking the skillet frequently. Add the garlic and cook for 1 minute. Discard the garlic.

Stir 1/3 cup of the walnuts into the zucchini mixture and cook just until warm. Season to taste with salt and pepper. Spoon the zucchini mixture into a serving bowl and sprinkle with the remaining walnuts. Garnish with chopped fresh parsley, if desired. *Yield: 6 servings.*

Sweet Potato Muffins

1 3/4 cups all-purpose flour
2 tablespoons brown sugar
1 tablespoon baking powder
1 teaspoon salt
1/2 cup chopped pecans
1 cup (2 sticks) butter or margarine, melted
3/4 cup milk
2 eggs
1 1/2 cups mashed cooked sweet potatoes
1 tablespoon ground cinnamon
1 tablespoon granulated sugar

Sift the flour, brown sugar, baking powder and salt into a bowl and mix well. Stir in the pecans. Whisk the butter, milk and eggs in a bowl until blended and stir in the sweet potatoes. Add to the flour mixture and stir just until moistened.

Fill greased 2-inch muffin cups two-thirds full. Sprinkle the tops lightly with a mixture of the cinnamon and granulated sugar. Bake in a preheated 375-degree oven for 30 to 35 minutes or until the muffins test done. Cool in the pan for 2 minutes. Remove to a wire rack. *Yield: 18 muffins.*

Sweet Potato Soufflé

4 cups mashed cooked sweet potatoes
1 cup chopped peanuts or pecans
1 cup raisins
1/2 cup packed light brown sugar
1 egg, lightly beaten
8 (about) large marshmallows (optional)

Combine the sweet potatoes, peanuts, raisins, brown sugar and egg in a bowl and mix well. Spoon into a greased 8- to 10-inch baking dish. Bake in a preheated 375-degree oven until light brown. Top with the marshmallows and cook just until the marshmallows turn light brown. *Yield: 6 servings.*

Speedy Sweet Potatoes

2 (16-ounce) cans sweet potatoes, drained
1/2 teaspoon salt (optional)
1 (8-ounce) can crushed pineapple, drained
1/4 cup coarsely chopped pecans
1 tablespoon brown sugar
1 cup miniature marshmallows
Ground nutmeg to taste

Layer the sweet potatoes, salt, pineapple, pecans, brown sugar and 1/2 cup of the marshmallows in the order listed in a 1 1/2-quart microwave-safe dish. Microwave, covered, on High for 5 to 7 minutes or until bubbly around the edges. Sprinkle with the remaining 1/2 cup marshmallows. Microwave, uncovered, on High for 1 to 2 minutes or until the marshmallows puff. Sprinkle with nutmeg and serve immediately. *Yield: 6 servings.*

Bacon and Cherry Tomato Bites

4 slices bacon
18 firm cherry tomatoes
1/2 cup mayonnaise
1/4 cup (1 ounce) grated Parmesan cheese
1 green onion, finely chopped

Cook the bacon in a skillet until brown and crisp; drain. Cool slightly and crumble. Slice the tops off the tomatoes and scoop out the pulp and seeds. Cut a very thin slice off the bottoms of the tomatoes to allow them to stand upright. Invert onto paper towels to drain.

Combine the mayonnaise, cheese and green onions in a bowl and mix well. Stir in the bacon. Fill each tomato with a spoonful of the mayonnaise mixture. Arrange the stuffed tomatoes on a platter and chill, covered, until serving time. *Yield: 6 (3-tomato) servings.*

Crostini with Fresh Tomato Basil Topping

1 (9-ounce) loaf French or Italian bread (20 inches long)
1 1/4 cups prepared hummus
1 large fully ripened fresh Florida tomato, seeded and chopped (about 1 cup)
1/4 cup chopped black olives
1/4 cup chopped fresh basil leaves, or 1 tablespoon dried basil
2 tablespoons balsamic vinaigrette or Italian salad dressing
1 teaspoon finely chopped garlic

Cut the loaf diagonally into 1-inch slices and arrange the slices cut side down in a single layer in a shallow baking pan. Toast in a preheated 450-degree oven for 2 minutes on each side. Spread about 1 tablespoon of the hummus on each slice.

Combine the tomato, olives, basil, vinaigrette and garlic in a bowl and mix well. Top the bread slices with equal amounts of the tomato mixture. Garnish each with a cooked small shrimp or sliver of prosciutto, if desired. Serve immediately. You may substitute 1 1/2 cups crumbled feta cheese for the hummus. Press the feta cheese onto the toasted bread slices. *Yield: 20 servings.*

Citrus-Marinated Tomato Salad over Steak

1/4 cup Italian salad dressing
1/2 teaspoon grated orange or lemon zest
1 pound fully ripened fresh Florida tomatoes, chopped (about 2 1/2 cups)
1 (6- to 8-ounce) package yellow or Spanish rice mix
1 teaspoon salt
1 teaspoon ground cumin
1/4 teaspoon ground pepper
4 (4-ounce) beef round cube steaks, pounded thin
2 teaspoons olive oil
12 ounces mixed salad greens

Mix the salad dressing and orange zest in a bowl. Add the tomatoes and toss gently. Let stand for 15 minutes. Prepare the rice using the package directions.

Mix the salt, cumin and pepper in a bowl. Rub over the surface of the steaks. Heat 1 teaspoon of the olive oil in a large nonstick skillet over medium-high heat. Cook the steaks two at a time in the hot oil for 1 1/2 minutes per side for medium or until brown on both sides and cooked to the desired degree of doneness, turning once. Add the remaining 1 teaspoon olive oil as needed.

Divide the rice evenly among four serving plates and top each serving with one steak, one-fourth of the salad greens and one-fourth of the tomato mixture. Serve immediately.
Yield: 4 servings.

GROWING TOMATOES IN FLORIDA

Like the sunny Mediterranean region, Florida has the warm temperatures necessary for cultivating tomatoes. Tomato plants are started in greenhouses and the seedlings are transplanted to fields about five weeks later. One pound of seed produces up to 140,000 plants. Tomatoes are harvested by hand roughly 100 to 120 days after planting. At the mature green stage, they have reached their full size and contain virtually all of the vitamins and nutrients of fully ripened tomatoes.

The Florida tomato industry is the nation's largest producer of fresh tomatoes, growing virtually all the fresh-market, field-grown tomatoes in the United States from October through June of each year.

Florida Sun and Sea Chef Salad

2 large fully ripened fresh Florida tomatoes (about 1 pound)
2 oranges, peeled
$^1/_3$ cup prepared vinaigrette
4 cups packed mixed salad greens or lettuce leaves
12 ounces deveined peeled cooked shrimp (about $1^1/_2$ cups)
1 green bell pepper, thinly sliced
4 ounces goat cheese, crumbled (1 cup)

Core and cut each tomato into twelve wedges. Cut each orange crosswise into six slices and cut the slices into halves. Process eight of the tomato wedges and four of the end orange slices in a blender or food processor for 1 minute or until smooth. Add the vinaigrette and process until blended and of a dressing consistency.

Place 1 cup of the salad greens on each of four chilled salad plates. Top each serving with equal amounts of the tomato wedges, orange slices, shrimp, bell pepper and goat cheese. Drizzle each salad with some of the dressing. Serve with the remaining dressing. *Yield: 4 servings.*

The nutritional profile includes all of the dressing.

Tomato Spinach Dip

1 (10-ounce) package frozen spinach, thawed and drained
8 ounces cream cheese, softened
$^1/_3$ cup milk
$^1/_4$ teaspoon salt
$^1/_4$ teaspoon cayenne pepper
2 fully ripened fresh Florida tomatoes, chopped
1 small onion, finely chopped

Press the excess moisture from the spinach. Beat the cream cheese, milk, salt and cayenne pepper in a mixing bowl until smooth. Stir in the spinach, tomatoes and onion.

Spoon into an ungreased baking dish. Bake in a preheated 375-degree oven until hot and bubbly. Serve immediately with assorted party crackers and/or garlic bread. *Yield: 8 servings.*

Tomatoes and Eggs Alfredo

2 large fully ripened fresh Florida tomatoes (about 1 pound)
1/2 teaspoon dried thyme
1/4 teaspoon salt
3/4 cup prepared Alfredo sauce
6 eggs, lightly beaten, or equivalent amount of egg substitute
2 English muffins, split and toasted
8 slices (8 ounces) bacon, crisp-cooked and drained

Core the tomatoes. Cut two thick slices from the center of each tomato. Chop the remaining portions of the tomatoes. The chopped tomatoes should measure about 1 3/4 cups. Sprinkle both sides of the tomato slices with the thyme and salt. Heat the Alfredo sauce in a saucepan using the package directions. Cover to keep warm.

Combine the eggs and chopped tomatoes in a bowl and mix well. Pour into a medium nonstick skillet. Cook, covered, for 5 minutes or until set; do not stir. Cut the egg mixture into quarters.

Arrange one muffin half on each of four serving plates. Layer each muffin half with 1 tablespoon of the Alfredo sauce, two slices of the bacon, one-fourth of the egg mixture, 2 tablespoons of the remaining Alfredo sauce and one tomato slice. Garnish with a sprig of your favorite herb, if desired. Serve immediately. *Yield: 4 servings.*

ENJOY A FLORIDA TOMATO TODAY FOR A HEALTHIER TOMORROW

Florida tomatoes have more going for them than just good looks and great taste—the redness that signals ripeness also means that they are rich in lycopene, an antioxidant that emerging research suggests helps prevent certain cancers and preserve heart health.
In addition, fresh tomatoes are a source of essential nutrients, including vitamins A and C, potassium, and fiber.
While the disease-fighting benefits of tomatoes are most often attributed to lycopene, many researchers are beginning to conclude that this antioxidant works in close partnership with other nutrients and antioxidants in tomatoes.

Tomato, Shrimp and Couscous Salad

1 (6-ounce) package roasted garlic couscous
8 ounces deveined peeled cooked shrimp
2 fully ripened fresh Florida tomatoes, cut into wedges
1 yellow bell pepper, chopped
1/2 cup Italian salad dressing
1/2 cup crumbled feta cheese
1/4 cup sliced green onions or scallions

Prepare the couscous using the package directions. Let stand until cool. Combine the shrimp, tomatoes, bell pepper and 1/4 cup of the salad dressing in a bowl and mix gently. Marinate, covered, in the refrigerator. Combine the couscous, feta cheese, green onions and remaining 1/4 cup salad dressing in a bowl and mix gently. Mound the couscous mixture evenly on four serving plates. Top each serving with one-fourth of the shrimp mixture. *Yield: 4 servings.*

Tomato and Squash Tart

2 large fully ripened fresh Florida tomatoes (about 1 pound)
2 large zucchini and/or yellow summer squash (about 1 pound)
1 (6-ounce) potato, peeled
1/4 cup chopped onion
2 eggs, lightly beaten
3/4 cup (3 ounces) shredded Swiss cheese
1 teaspoon salt
1/2 teaspoon Italian seasoning
1/4 teaspoon ground pepper
1/4 cup (1 ounce) shredded Swiss cheese

Remove the stem ends from the tomatoes. Cut the tomatoes through the stem ends into halves. Cut the halves crosswise into thin slices. Cut the zucchini and potato lengthwise into halves. Cut the halves crosswise into thin slices.

Combine the zucchini, potato, onion, eggs, 3/4 cup cheese, the salt, Italian seasoning and pepper in a bowl and mix well. Arrange half the tomato slices over the bottom of a 9-inch pie plate or shallow baking dish sprayed with nonstick cooking spray. Spoon the zucchini mixture over the tomatoes, pressing lightly to flatten. Top with the remaining tomato halves and sprinkle with 1/4 cup cheese. Bake in a preheated 400-degree oven for about 40 minutes. *Yield: 8 servings.*

Tortilla Pizzas with Roasted Tomatoes

1 1/2 pounds fully ripened fresh Florida tomatoes, thinly sliced (3 large tomatoes)
2 small onions, thinly sliced
1 tablespoon vegetable oil
4 flour tortillas
1 1/2 cups (6 ounces) coarsely shredded Pepper Jack cheese or Monterey Jack cheese

Arrange the tomato slices and onion slices in a single layer on a baking sheet. Brush with 2 teaspoons of the oil. Roast on the lowest oven rack in a preheated 425-degree oven for 10 minutes or until the tomatoes and onion are tender and golden brown. Remove to a platter. Maintain the oven temperature.

Wipe the baking sheet with a paper towel and brush the baking sheet with the remaining 1 teaspoon oil. Arrange the tortillas in a single layer on the prepared baking sheet. Sprinkle 3/4 cup of the cheese evenly over the tortillas and top with the roasted tomatoes and onions. Sprinkle with the remaining 3/4 cup cheese and bake for 8 minutes or until the tortilla edges are golden and crisp. Garnish with mixed salad greens, if desired. *Yield: 4 servings.*

Tropical Gazpacho Soup

1 (32-ounce) can low-sodium tomato juice
1 (20-ounce) can juice-pack crushed pineapple
1/2 cantaloupe, seeded and chopped
1 cucumber, peeled, seeded and chopped
1 bell pepper, chopped
1 papaya, chopped
1/4 cup Florida lime juice
1/4 cup Florida lemon juice
1 tablespoon chopped fresh parsley
1 1/2 teaspoons chopped fresh mint
1/4 teaspoon pepper
1/8 teaspoon hot red pepper sauce

Combine the tomato juice, undrained pineapple and cantaloupe in a blender and process until puréed. Pour into a large bowl. Stir in the cucumber, bell pepper and papaya. Add the lime juice, lemon juice, parsley, mint, pepper and hot sauce and mix well. Chill, covered, for 1 hour. Ladle into soup bowls. *Yield: 10 servings.*

THE FRUIT THAT ACTS LIKE A VEGETABLE

Botanically, the tomato is a fruit of the vine. In the kitchen, it is almost always treated as a vegetable. In fact, in 1893 the United States Supreme Court ruled, for the purpose of levying a tariff, that the tomato was a vegetable.

WINTER GAZPACHO OLÉ

- 1 1/2 pounds fully ripened fresh Florida tomatoes (about 3 large tomatoes)
- 1 tablespoon vegetable oil
- 1 1/2 teaspoons ground cumin
- 1 cup chopped green bell pepper
- 1/2 cup sliced scallions or green onions
- 4 cups mild picante-flavor vegetable juice
- 1 (19-ounce) can black beans, drained and rinsed
- 1/4 cup chopped fresh cilantro leaves
- 3/4 teaspoon salt

Core and chop the tomatoes. The chopped tomatoes should measure about 4 cups. Heat the oil in a saucepan until hot and stir in the cumin. Cook for 30 seconds or until fragrant, stirring constantly. Stir in the chopped tomatoes, bell pepper and scallions.

Cook for 3 to 5 minutes or until the bell pepper is tender-crisp, stirring occasionally. Add the vegetable juice, beans, cilantro and salt and cook for 3 to 5 minutes or until heated through, stirring occasionally. Ladle into soup bowls and garnish with a dollop of sour cream and additional chopped tomatoes and/or sliced radishes. *Yield: 6 servings.*

Greek Salad Pitas

2 fully ripened fresh Florida tomatoes (about 1 pound)
3 tablespoons olive oil
$1^1/_2$ tablespoons lemon juice
$1^1/_2$ teaspoons chopped fresh oregano, or $^1/_2$ teaspoon dried oregano
1 teaspoon sugar
$^1/_2$ teaspoon salt
$^2/_3$ cup chopped peeled cucumber
$^1/_3$ cup chopped green bell pepper
$^1/_4$ cup coarsely chopped black olives
2 tablespoons chopped red onion
4 (6-inch) pita rounds, heated
8 ounces hummus
4 leaves Boston or iceberg lettuce, cut into halves
3 ounces feta cheese, crumbled (about $^2/_3$ cup)

Cut each tomato into eight slices. Whisk the olive oil, lemon juice, oregano, sugar and salt in a bowl until combined. Add the cucumber, bell pepper, olives and onion and stir until coated. Cut the pita rounds into halves and open gently.

Spread equal amounts of the hummus in each pita pocket. Stuff each pita with one lettuce leaf half, two tomato slices and about $^1/_4$ cup of the cucumber mixture. Sprinkle evenly with the cheese. Serve immediately. *Yield: 4 servings.*

Veggie Christmas Tree

1 (8-ounce) bottle fat-free ranch salad dressing
4 cups broccoli florets, cut into bite-size pieces
1 broccoli stem
3 to 4 cups cauliflower florets, cut into bite-size pieces
4 or 5 cherry tomatoes, quartered
1 carrot, sliced

Cover the bottom of a 9×13-inch dish with the salad dressing. Arrange the broccoli florets in the shape of a tree in the prepared dish, using the broccoli stem as the tree trunk. Place the cauliflower florets around the tree. Decorate the tree with the tomatoes and carrots slices. *Yield: 20 servings.*

Tuscan Vegetable Lasagna

6 lasagna noodles
2 teaspoons olive oil
2 zucchini and/or yellow summer squash, cut lengthwise into halves and sliced
2 cups sliced fresh mushrooms
1 small onion, chopped
1 cup part-skim ricotta cheese
1/4 cup (1 ounce) grated Parmesan cheese
1/4 teaspoon ground pepper
2 cups pasta sauce
1 cup (4 ounces) shredded part-skim mozzarella cheese
1 fully ripened fresh Florida tomato, seeded and chopped

Cook the noodles using the package directions; drain. Rinse with cold water and drain. Heat the olive oil in a large nonstick skillet over medium heat. Stir in the zucchini, mushrooms and onion and cook for 5 minutes or until the vegetables are tender. Remove from the heat. Mix the ricotta cheese, Parmesan cheese and pepper in a bowl.

Arrange three of the noodles over the bottom of a shallow 2-quart baking dish, trimming to fit if needed. Layer with half the ricotta cheese mixture, half the zucchini mixture, 1 cup of the pasta sauce and 1/2 cup of the mozzarella cheese. Top with the remaining noodles, remaining ricotta cheese mixture, remaining zucchini mixture and remaining 1 cup pasta sauce.

Bake in a preheated 375-degree oven for 30 minutes. Sprinkle with the tomato and the remaining 1/2 cup mozzarella cheese. Bake for 5 minutes longer or until heated through. Let stand for 10 minutes before serving. *Yield: 6 servings.*

Veggie Pasta Primavera

1 pound fresh asparagus spears
8 ounces rotini
1 large red or yellow bell pepper, cut into 1-inch pieces
1 cup assorted fresh summer squash (sunburst squash halves, sliced zucchini and/or sliced yellow summer squash)
1 tablespoon butter
2 garlic cloves, minced
2 cups fat-free milk
3 tablespoons all-purpose flour
1/2 teaspoon salt
1 tablespoon snipped fresh tarragon or basil
1/4 teaspoon crushed red pepper
1/2 cup (2 ounces) grated Parmesan cheese

Snap off the thick woody ends of the asparagus spears and discard. Slice the asparagus into 1-inch pieces. Cook the pasta using the package directions, adding the asparagus, bell pepper and squash during the last 3 minutes of the cooking process; drain. Return the pasta and vegetables to the hot saucepan.

Melt the butter in a small saucepan over medium heat. Add the garlic and cook for 1 minute, stirring constantly. Whisk the milk, flour and salt in a bowl until blended. Stir into the garlic mixture and cook until thick and bubbly, stirring constantly. Decrease the temperature to low and cook for 1 minute longer. Stir in the tarragon and red pepper. Pour the sauce over the pasta mixture and toss gently to coat. Spoon equal amounts onto four serving plates and sprinkle with the cheese. *Yield: 4 servings.*

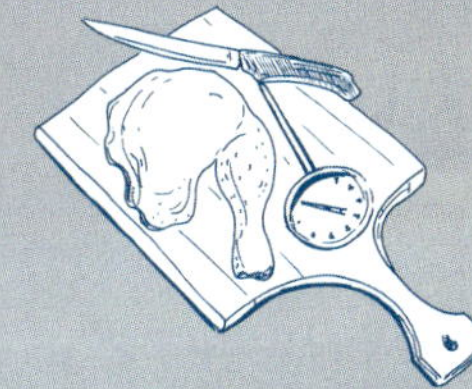

GARLIC

The Egyptian slaves are said to have built the pyramids on a diet of garlic, bread, and water. When selecting garlic, look for large, firm heads whose skins cling tightly to the bulb. Avoid old heads with greens sprouting out of the top or hollow spots. Store garlic in a cool, dry place such as a potato or onion bin or in the open air, never in the refrigerator where it will absorb moisture.

CHILDREN AND VEGETABLES

Those of us who enjoy vegetables know that children do not always share our love of broccoli, cauliflower, and brussels sprouts. Most young children prefer mild-tasting and slightly undercooked vegetables, and they want them served individually . . . peas OR carrots, rather than peas AND carrots! Most young children enjoy smooth vegetables, like mashed potatoes, but only if they are free of lumps.

Give children repeated opportunities to try new veggies and remember that it takes many contacts with new foods for children to be comfortable. Never "bribe" children to eat their veggies, since this teaches that vegetables are not good to eat without a reward, and we know better.

Vegetable Spaghetti Bake

8 ounces spaghetti
1 (28-ounce) jar meatless spaghetti sauce
1 tablespoon olive oil or canola oil
1½ cups (½-inch) pieces zucchini
1 cup sliced celery
1 cup thinly sliced carrots
1 cup sliced fresh mushrooms
1 onion, chopped
2 cups fat-free cottage cheese
2 cups (8 ounces) shredded part-skim mozzarella cheese
2 tablespoons grated Parmesan cheese

Cook the pasta using the package directions. Drain and place the pasta in a large bowl. Add 1½ cups of the spaghetti sauce and mix until coated. Heat the olive oil in a large nonstick skillet until hot and add the zucchini, celery, carrots, mushrooms and onion. Sauté until the vegetables are tender.

Spread ½ cup of the remaining spaghetti sauce in a 9×13-inch baking dish coated with nonstick cooking spray. Layer the pasta mixture, cottage cheese, vegetable mixture and mozzarella cheese one-half at a time in the prepared baking dish. Spread with the remaining spaghetti sauce and sprinkle with the Parmesan cheese.

Bake, covered, in a preheated 350-degree oven for 30 minutes. Remove the cover and bake for 10 to 15 minutes longer or until bubbly. Let stand for 10 minutes before serving. *Yield: 9 servings.*

Recipe Contributors

The list of contributors for the efforts in the production of *Simply Florida* is too extensive to list. However, we would like to thank the membership, staff, family, and friends of the Florida Extension Association of Family and Consumer Sciences for their time commitment, hard work, and tireless giving of their personal and professional time. We are truly grateful for their support, for without it, *Simply Florida* would still be a dream. Thank you.

Kathryn Allen
Louise Amdal
Linda Bobroff
Deborah Boulware
Linda Bowman
Monica Brinkley
Nettie Ruth Brown
Chef John Clark
Joanne Cooper
Heidi Copeland
Judith Corbus
Elaine Courtney
Herman Courtney
Betsy Crisp
Nonie Crom
Jean Cross
Monica Dawkins
Jan Devine
Duska Dorshel
Joan Elmore
Bonnie Fauls
Myron Felder
Florida Dairy Association
Florida Peanut Producers
Florida Poultry Federation
Florida Strawberry Growers
Florida Tomato Growers
Ruth Gaines
Danielle Gordon
Roberta Hall
Betty Hayner
Teisha Hicks
Celia Hill
Sarah Hink
Barry Hoover
Barbara Hughes
Dr. Freddie Johnson
Ronnie Johnson
Ruby Johnson
Kathy Kay
Mary Keith
Samantha Kennedy
Bertha Kimball
Gus Koerner
Rita Law-McCumber
Curtis Lee
Lisa Leslie
Corey Lovell
Michelle Lynch
Rona Lynch
Theda Mack
Brenda Marty-Jimenez
Mildred Melvin
Betty Miller
Karl Mohler
Marjorie Moore
Carol O'Connell
Mary Joe Oswald
Angela Pasko
Suzanne Pearson
Mary Peters
Caroline Pollock
Executive Chef Jeannie Purola
Beverly Roberge
Janet Rodriguez-Collura
Brenda Rogers
Mary Beth Salisbury
Jacqueline Schrader
Reva Searl
Elizabeth Shephard
Jo Shuford-Law
Mary Young Smith
Wynn Sommers
Chef Rocky Tarantello
Meredith Taylor
Dr. Nayda Torres
Jamie Verge
Cheryl Vergot
Brenda H. Walters
Wanda Walters
Jared Watson
R.J. Webb
Gayle Whitworth
Brenda Williams
Tativna Williams

Special Acknowledgments

We would like to thank Dairy Management, Inc., Florida Tomato Growers Association, and Florida Strawberry Growers Association for contributing the following recipes to *Simply Florida*.

Baked Pears with Vanilla Yogurt and Granola (page 76)—Recipe created by 3-A-Day™ of Dairy

Baked Spinach Artichoke Dip (page 65)—Recipe created by 3-A-Day™ of Dairy

Breakfast Smoothie (page 70)—Recipe created by 3-A-Day™ of Dairy

Caramelized Grilled Strawberries and Ice Cream (page 126)—Recipe created by Florida Strawberry Growers Association

*Cheese Lover's Pizza Square*s (page 66)—Recipe created by 3-A-Day™ of Dairy

Cheesy Baked Chicken (page 36)—Recipe created for 3-A-Day™ of Dairy by Habni Nutrition Consultants, creators of the Soul Food Pyramid

Chicken with Spanish-Style Rice and Tomatoes (page 42)—Recipe created by Florida Tomato Committee

Choco-Nana Milk Mixer (page 68)—Recipe created by Elizabeth Ward, M.S., R.D., and author of *Healthy Foods, Healthy Kids*

Citrus-Marinated Tomato Salad Over Steak (page 153)—Recipe created by Florida Tomato Committee

Confetti Quesadillas with Cilantro Yogurt Dip (page 67)—Recipe created by 3-A-Day™ of Dairy

Crostini with Fresh Tomato Basil Topping (page 152)—Recipe created by Florida Tomato Committee

Special Acknowledgments

Peanut Butter Squares (page 90)—Recipe created by Florida Peanut Producers

Festive Fruity Flavored Milk (page 69)—Recipe created by 3-A-Day™ of Dairy

Fresh Berry-Stuffed French Toast with Yogurt Sauce (page 110)—Recipe created on behalf of 3-A-Day™ of Dairy by Chef Federico Elbl of Palermo Viejo, Louisville, Kentucky

Frozen Peanut Butter Pie (page 90)—Recipe created by Florida Peanut Producers

Greek Salad Pitas (page 159)—Recipe created by Florida Tomato Committee

Roasted Strawberry and Tomato Soup (page 128)—Recipe created by Florida Strawberry Growers Association

Shrimp and Spinach Pita Pizzas (page 61)—Recipe courtesy of Sargento®

Strawberry Yogurt Shortcake (page 79)—Recipe created by Yoplait®

Strawberry Yogurt Smoothie (page 71)—Recipe used with permission of Kraft Foods®

Tomatoes and Eggs Alfredo (page 155)—Recipe created by Florida Tomato Committee

Tomato, Shrimp and Couscous Salad (page 156)—Recipe created by Florida Tomato Committee

Turkey Cheddar Wrap with Spiced Yogurt Dip (page 45)—Recipe created by 3-A-Day™ of Dairy

Vanilla-Grilled Lobster with Florida Strawberry, Fennel and Pistachio Salad and Tangerine Butter (page 129)—Recipe created by Florida Strawberry Growers Association

Winter Gazpacho Olé (page 158)—Recipe created by Florida Tomato Committee

Resources

Dairy Farmers, Inc.
www.floridamilk.com
166 Lookout Place, Suite 100
Maitland, FL 32751
Phone: (407) 647-8899
Fax: (407) 647-0606

Florida Tomato Committee
www.floridatomatoes.com
800 Trafalgar Court, Suite 300
Maitland, FL 32751
Phone: (407) 660-1949
Fax: (407) 660-1656

County Extension Offices
www.solutionsforyourlife.com

DISTRICT 1 (NORTHWEST FLORIDA)

Bay County
647 Jenks Avenue, Suite A
Panama City, FL 32401-2660
(850) 784-6105

Calhoun County
20816 Central Avenue E, Suite 1
Blountstown, FL 32424-2276
(850) 674-8323

Escambia County
3740 Stefani Road
Cantonment, FL 32533-7792
(850) 475-5230

Franklin County
66 4th Street
Apalachicola, FL 32320-1775
(850) 653-9337

Gadsden County
2140 W Jefferson Street
Quincy, FL 32351-1905
(850) 875-7255

Gulf County
200 N 2nd Street
P.O. Box 250
Wewahitchka, FL 32465
(850) 639-3200

Holmes County
201 N Oklahoma Street, Suite 3
Bonifay, FL 32425-2295
(850) 547-1108

Jackson County
2741 Pennsylvania Avenue, Suite 3
Marianna, FL 32448-4022
(850) 482-9620

Jefferson County
275 N Mulberry Street
Monticello, FL 32344-2249
(850) 342-0187

Leon County
615 Paul Russell Road
Tallahassee, FL 32301-7060
(850) 487-3003

Resources

Liberty County
10405 NW Theo Jacobs Way
P.O. Box 369
Bristol, FL 32321
(850) 643-2229

Madison County
184 NW College Loop
Madison, FL 32340-1426
(850) 973-4138

Okaloosa County
5479 Old Bethel Road
Crestview, FL 32536-5512
(850) 689-5850

Santa Rosa County
6263 Dogwood Drive
Milton, FL 32570-3500
(850) 623-3868

Taylor County
203 Forest Park Drive
Perry, FL 32348-6340
(850) 838-3508

Wakulla County
84 Cedar Avenue
Crawfordville, FL 32327-2063
(850) 926-3931

Walton County
732 N 9th Street, Suite B
DeFuniak Springs, FL 32433-3804
(850) 892-8172

Washington County
1424 Jackson Avenue, Suite A
Chipley, FL 32428-1602
(850) 638-6180

DISTRICT 2
(NORTHEAST FLORIDA)

Alachua County
2800 NE 39th Avenue
Gainesville, FL 32609-2658
(352) 955-2402

Baker County
1025 W Macclenny Avenue
Macclenny, FL 32063-9640
(904) 259-3520

Bradford County
2266 N Temple Avenue
Starke, FL 32091-1612
(904) 966-6224

Clay County
2463 State Route 16 W
P.O. Box 278
Green Cove Springs, FL 32043
(904) 284-6355

Columbia County
164 SW Mary Ethel Lane
Lake City, FL 32025
(386) 752-5384

Resources

Dixie County
214 NE 351 Highway
P.O. Box 640
Cross City, FL 32628
(352) 498-1237

Duval County
1010 N McDuff Avenue
Jacksonville, FL 32254-2031
(904) 387-8850

Flagler County
150 Sawgrass Road
Bunnell, FL 32110-4325
(386) 437-7464

Gilchrist County
125 East Wade Street
P.O. Box 157
Trenton, FL 32693
(352) 463-3174

Hamilton County
1143 U.S. Highway 41 NW
Jasper, FL 32052-5856
(386) 792-1276

Lafayette County
176 SW Community Circle,
Suite D
Mayo, FL 32066-4000
(386) 294-1279

Levy County
625 N Hathaway Avenue
Alternate 27
P.O. Box 219
Bronson, FL 32621-0219
(352) 486-5131

Nassau County
543350 U.S. Highway 1
Callahan, FL 32011-6486
(904) 879-1019

Putnam County
111 Yelvington Road, Suite 1
East Palatka, FL 32131-2114
(386) 329-0318

St. Johns County
3125 Agricultural Center Drive
St. Augustine, FL 32092-0572
(904) 209-0430

Suwannee County
1302 11th Street SW
Live Oak, FL 32060-3611
(386) 362-2771

Union County
25 NE 1st Street
Lake Butler, FL 32054-1701
(386) 496-2321

Resources

DISTRICT 3 (CENTRAL FLORIDA)

Brevard County
3695 Lake Drive
Cocoa, FL 32926-4219
(321) 633-1702

1455 Treeland Boulevard SE
Palm Bay, FL 32909-2212
(321) 952-4536

Citrus County
3650 W Sovereign Path, Suite 1
Lecanto, FL 34461
(352) 527-5700

Hernando County
19490 Oliver Street
Brooksville, FL 34601-6538
(352)754-4433

Lake County
30205 State Route 19
Tavares, FL 32778-4204
(352) 343-4101

Marion County
2232 NE Jacksonville Road
Ocala, FL 34470-3615
(352) 671-8400

Orange County
2350 E Michigan Street
Orlando, FL 32806-4939
(407) 836-7570

Osceola County
Osceola Heritage Park
1921 Kissimmee Valley Lane,
Suite A
Kissimmee, FL 34744-6107
(321) 697-3000

Pasco County
36702 State Route 52
Dade City, FL 33525-5138
(352) 521-4288

Polk County
1702 Highway 17 South
Bartow, FL 33830
(863) 519-8677

Seminole County
250 W County Home Road
Sanford, FL 32773-6189
(407) 665-5551

Sumter County
7620 State Route 471, Suite 2
Bushnell, FL 33513
(352) 793-2728

Resources

Volusia County
3100 E New York Avenue
DeLand, FL 32724-6497
(386) 822-5778

DISTRICT 4
(SOUTH CENTRAL FLORIDA)

Charlotte County
25550 Harbor View Road, Unit 3
Port Charlotte, FL 33980-2503
(941) 764-4340

Collier County
14700 Immokalee Road
Naples, FL 34120-1468
(239) 353-4244

Desoto County
2150 NE Roan Street
P.O. Box 310
Arcadia, FL 34266-0310
(863) 993-4846

Glades County
900 U.S. Highway 27 SW
P.O. Box 549
Moore Haven, FL 33471
(863) 946-0244

Hardee County
507 Civic Center Drive
Wauchula, FL 33873-9460
(863) 773-2164

Highlands County
4509 W George Boulevard
Sebring, FL 33875-5837
(863) 402-6540

Hillsborough County
5339 S County Road 579
Seffner, FL 33584-3334
(813) 744-5519

Lee County
3406 Palm Beach Boulevard
Fort Myers, FL 33916-3736
(239) 461-7500

Manatee County
1303 17th Street W
Palmetto, FL 34221-2998
(941) 722-4524

Okeechobee County
458 Highway 98 N
Okeechobee, FL 34972-2303
(863) 763-6469

Pinellas County
12175 125th Street N
Largo, FL 33774-3612
(727) 582-2100

Sarasota County
6700 Clark Road
Sarasota, FL 34241-9328
(941) 861-9808

Resources

DISTRICT 5
(SOUTH FLORIDA)

Broward County
3245 College Avenue
Davie, FL 33314-7798
(954) 370-3725

Hendry County
1085 Pratt Boulevard
Labelle, FL 33935
(863) 674-4092

Indian River County
1028 20th Place, Suite D
Vero Beach, FL 32960-5360
(772) 770-5030

Martin County
2614 SE Dixie Highway
Stuart, FL 34996-4007
(772) 288-5654

Miami-Dade County
18710 SW 288th Street
Homestead, FL 33030-2309
(305) 248-3311

Blanch-Morton Center
City of Hialeah
300 E 1st Avenue, Room 113
Hialeah, FL 33010-4808
(305) 888-5010

Miami International Mall—4-H
1455 NW 107th Avenue, Suite 906
Miami, FL 33172-2721
(305) 592-8049

Sea Grant Office
4600 Rickenbacker Causeway
Key Biscayne, FL 33149
(305) 361-4017

Monroe County
1100 Siminton Street,
Room 2-206
Key West, FL 33040-3110
(305) 292-4501

Palm Beach County
559 N Military Trail
West Palm Beach, FL 33415-1311
(561) 233-1712

345 S Congress Avenue
Delray Beach, FL 33445
(561) 276-1263

2976 State Route 15
Belle Glade, FL 33430-5300
(561) 996-1655

St. Lucie County
8400 Picos Road, Suite 101
Fort Pierce, FL 34945-3045
(772) 462-1660

Ingredient Equivalents

Making a shopping list based on the ingredients of a recipe can be tricky if you don't know how many tomatoes will yield 3 cups of chopped tomatoes. Using these guidelines will help determine what you will need.

INGREDIENT	EQUIVALENT
1 cup sliced apple	1 large apple
1 cup mashed banana	3 medium bananas
3 1/4 to 4 cups berries	1 quart berries
3 cups whole cherries or 2 1/2 cups halves	1 pound cherries
4 1/2 cups shredded cabbage	1 small head cabbage (1 pound)
1 cup grated carrot	1 large carrot
1 cup diced or chopped celery	2 medium stalks celery
1 cup semisweet chocolate pieces	6-ounce package semisweet chocolate pieces
1 cup shredded hard cheese (Cheddar, Swiss)	4 ounces hard cheese
3/4 cup grated cheese (Parmesan, Romano)	1/4 pound hard cheese
2 cups whipped cream	1 cup unwhipped cream
1 cup cream cheese	8-ounce package cream cheese
1 cup soft bread crumbs	1 1/2 to 2 slices bread
1 cup dry bread crumbs	4 slices bread
1 cup graham cracker crumbs	10 graham cracker squares
1 cup finely crushed vanilla wafer crumbs	30 vanilla wafers
1 cup finely crushed gingersnap crumbs	15 gingersnaps
3 cups sliced raw mushrooms	3/4 pound raw mushrooms
4 cups chopped pecans or walnuts	1 pound shelled pecans or walnuts
1/2 cup chopped onion	1 medium onion
1 cup diced green pepper	1 large green pepper
3 cups cooked rice	1 cup uncooked rice
3 cups whole strawberries or 1 cup sliced	1 pint strawberries (about 1 pound)
1 cup chopped tomato	1 large tomato

Baking Dish Equivalents

PAN TYPE AND SIZE	VOLUME
Loaf Pans	
$5^{1}/_{2}$×3×$2^{1}/_{2}$-inch	2 cups
6×$4^{1}/_{2}$×3-inch	3 cups
8×4×$2^{1}/_{2}$-inch	4 cups
$8^{1}/_{2}$×$4^{1}/_{4}$×3-inch	5 cups
9×5×3-inch	8 cups
Tube Pans	
$7^{1}/_{2}$×3-inch bundt	6 cups
9×3-inch bundt	9 cups
10×$3^{1}/_{2}$-inch bundt	12 cups
8×3-inch tube	9 cups
9×3-inch tube	10 cups
10×4-inch tube	16 cups
9×4-inch kugelhopf	11 cups
Layer/Cake Pans	
6×2-inch round	$3^{3}/_{4}$ cups
8×$1^{1}/_{2}$-inch round	4 cups
7×2-inch round	$5^{1}/_{4}$ cups
8×2-inch round	6 cups
9×2-inch round	8 cups
8×$1^{1}/_{2}$-inch square	6 cups
9×$1^{1}/_{2}$-inch square	8 cups
9×2-inch square	10 cups
10×2-inch square	11 cups
11×7×2-inch rectangle	9 cups
13×9×2-inch rectangle	15 cups

Ingredient Substitutions

Have you ever been all set to prepare a favorite dish and suddenly discover one of the ingredients in your recipe is missing? Listed below are suggested substitutions that can be used. Remember, however, that results may not be exact and may vary.

INGREDIENT	AMOUNT	SUBSTITUTIONS
Baking powder	1 teaspoon	1/4 teaspoon baking soda plus 5/8 teaspoon cream of tartar 1/4 teaspoon baking soda plus 1/2 cup sour milk or buttermilk (if using this, decrease amount of liquid called for in recipe by 1/2 cup)
Beef broth or chicken broth	1 (14 1/2-ounce) can	2 teaspoons instant beef or chicken bouillon granules with water to equal amount of broth needed
Bouillon cube	1	1 tablespoon soy sauce
Dry bread crumbs	1/4 cup	1/4 cup cracker crumbs or cornmeal 1 cup soft bread crumbs
Butter	1 cup	7/8 to 1 cup shortening plus 1/2 teaspoon salt 1 cup margarine
Chili sauce or ketchup	1 cup	1 cup tomato sauce plus 1/2 cup sugar and 2 tablespoons vinegar (for use in cooking only)
Chocolate chips, semisweet	1 ounce	1 ounce sweet cooking chocolate
Cornstarch	1 tablespoon	2 tablespoons all-purpose flour 2 tablespoons quick-cooking tapioca
Corn syrup	1 cup	1 cup sugar plus 1/4 cup liquid (use the type of liquid that is called for in the recipe)
Egg (cake batter only)	1	2 tablespoons mayonnaise
Flour, all-purpose	1 tablespoon	1/2 tablespoon cornstarch or quick-cooking tapioca (for thickening)

Ingredient Substitutions

INGREDIENT	AMOUNT	SUBSTITUTIONS
Flour, all-purpose	1 cup, sifted	1 cup plus 2 tablespoons sifted cake flour 1 cup unsifted all-purpose flour minus 2 tablespoons
Flour, cake	1 cup, sifted	1 cup minus 2 tablespoons sifted all-purpose flour
Garlic	1 small clove	1/8 teaspoon garlic powder
Gelatin, flavored	3-ounce package (prepared with water)	1 tablespoon plain gelatin plus 2 cups fruit juice
Herbs, fresh	1 tablespoon	1 teaspoon dried herbs
Honey	1 cup	1 1/2 cups sugar plus 1/4 cup liquid (use liquid called for in recipe)
Lemon	1 medium	2 to 3 tablespoons lemon juice and 1 to 2 teaspoons lemon zest
Lemon juice	1 teaspoon	1/2 teaspoon vinegar (for use as acid source in cooking only)
Milk, buttermilk	1 cup	1 cup yogurt 1 cup sour milk (1 tablespoon vinegar or lemon juice plus enough sweet milk to make 1 cup. Allow to stand for 5 to 10 minutes before using.)
Milk, skim	1 cup	5 tablespoons nonfat dry milk plus 1 cup water
Milk, whole	1 cup	1/2 cup evaporated milk plus 1 cup water
Mustard, prepared	1 tablespoon	1 teaspoon dried mustard
Onion, fresh	1 small	1 tablespoon dried minced onion, rehydrated
Parsley, dried	1 teaspoon	3 teaspoons chopped fresh parsley
Shortening, melted	1 cup	1 cup vegetable oil
Sour cream	1 cup	1 cup yogurt

Ingredient Substitutions

INGREDIENT	AMOUNT	SUBSTITUTIONS
Sugar, white	1 cup	1 cup corn syrup minus 1/4 cup liquid in recipe 1 cup brown sugar (firmly packed) 1 cup honey (reduce liquid in recipe by 1/4 cup) 1 3/4 cups confectioners' (powdered) sugar, packed
Tomatoes	1 (16-ounce) can	3 fresh medium tomatoes, chopped
Tomato juice	1 cup	1/2 cup tomato sauce plus 1/2 cup water
Tomato sauce	1 (15-ounce) can	1 (6-ounce) can tomato paste plus 1 cup water
Yogurt	1 cup	1 cup buttermilk 1 cup sour milk (1 tablespoon vinegar or lemon juice plus enough sweet milk to make 1 cup. Allow to stand for 5 to 10 minutes before using.)

Produce Buying Guide

Use this chart to help you in selecting your favorite Florida produce in season. Bananas, limes, mushrooms, okra, onions, and papaya are available year-round.

	JAN	FEB	MAR	APR	MAY	JUN	JUL	AUG	SEP	OCT	NOV	DEC
Avocado	✓	✓	✓			✓	✓	✓	✓	✓	✓	✓
Asian Pear							✓	✓	✓	✓		
Atemoya								✓	✓	✓		
Blackberries					✓	✓	✓	✓	✓			
Blueberries				✓	✓	✓						
Broccoli	✓	✓	✓	✓	✓							
Cabbage	✓	✓	✓	✓	✓	✓					✓	✓
Canistel	✓	✓	✓								✓	✓
Cantaloupe			✓	✓	✓	✓	✓					
Carambola	✓	✓	✓					✓	✓	✓	✓	✓
Carrots	✓	✓	✓	✓	✓	✓					✓	✓
Cauliflower	✓	✓	✓	✓	✓						✓	✓
Celery	✓	✓	✓	✓	✓	✓					✓	✓
Chinese Cabbage	✓	✓	✓	✓	✓	✓					✓	✓
Cucumbers	✓	✓	✓	✓	✓	✓					✓	✓
Eggplant	✓	✓	✓	✓	✓	✓			✓	✓	✓	✓
Endive/Escarole	✓	✓	✓	✓	✓	✓	✓			✓	✓	✓
Grapefruit	✓	✓	✓	✓	✓	✓	✓			✓	✓	✓
Grapes								✓	✓			
Guava	✓	✓			✓	✓	✓	✓	✓	✓		
Honeydew	✓	✓	✓	✓	✓						✓	✓

Produce Buying Guide

	JAN	FEB	MAR	APR	MAY	JUN	JUL	AUG	SEP	OCT	NOV	DEC
Kumquat	✓	✓	✓	✓	✓							✓
Mamey Sapote	✓	✓	✓	✓								
Mangoes						✓	✓	✓	✓			
Oranges	✓	✓	✓	✓	✓	✓	✓			✓	✓	✓
Passion Fruit	✓	✓	✓				✓	✓	✓	✓	✓	✓
Peppers	✓	✓	✓	✓	✓	✓	✓			✓	✓	✓
Potatoes	✓	✓	✓	✓	✓	✓	✓					
Pummelo	✓	✓									✓	✓
Radishes	✓	✓	✓	✓	✓	✓				✓	✓	✓
Spinach		✓	✓									
Squash	✓	✓	✓	✓	✓	✓			✓	✓	✓	✓
Strawberries	✓	✓	✓	✓	✓						✓	✓
Sweet Corn	✓	✓	✓	✓	✓	✓	✓		✓	✓	✓	✓
Tangerines/Tangelos	✓	✓	✓	✓					✓	✓	✓	✓
Tomatoes	✓	✓	✓	✓	✓	✓	✓		✓	✓	✓	✓
Watermelon	✓			✓	✓	✓	✓					✓

Nutritional Guidelines and Profiles

Nutritional information for recipes in this book was computed using the ***Food Processor SQL*** nutrition software. The database contains more than 29,000 foods for the use in analysis. More than 1,300 scientific sources of nutrition information were researched to compile the database. However, many specialty items, new products, and processed foods may not be available from the sources. In such cases, the most similar item was selected for inclusion in the analysis. More information on new and/or specific products may be obtained by reading those product nutrient labels.

Unless otherwise specified, the nutritional profiles adhere to the following considerations:

- Recipe ingredients are based on all measurements being level unless otherwise specified.
- Products are available commercially in the size and weights used.
- Canned items have been analyzed as "drained" unless the recipe specifically calls for including the liquid.
- The cooking method for any recipe is the same method used in the analysis.
- The fat content for ground beef is 10% for the "lean" designation.
- Eggs are large.
- Margarine and butter are solid or semi-solid form, not whipped or pre-softened.
- The percentage of butterfat is indicated for most fluid products. If the percentage of butterfat is not specified in the recipe, 2% milk and dairy products are used in the analysis. Evaporated milk is whole milk with 60% of the water removed.
- Oil is any type of vegetable cooking oil.
- Ingredients "to taste" have not been included in the nutritional profile.
- If a choice of ingredients has been suggested, the profile reflects the first option.
- If a choice of amounts has been given, the profile reflects the greatest amount.
- Garnishes, serving suggestions, and other optional information are not included in the profile.
- To calculate the percent (%) of calories from fat in a recipe, divide the number given for total fat calories by the number given for calories. Persons with dietary or health problems or whose diets require close monitoring should not rely solely on the nutritional information provided. They should consult their physician or a registered dietitian for specific information.

Nutritional Profiles

Pg. #	Recipe Title (Approx Per Serving)	Cal	Cal from Fat	T Fat (g)	Chol (mg)	Sod (mg)	Carbo (g)	Fiber (g)	Prot (g)
13	Beef Rib-Eye Roast with Savory Sauce	440	280	31	130	330	1	0	38
14	Chuck Roast Barbecue	840	430	48	190	920	41	2	58
15	Best Beef Brisket	360	150	17	140	780	1	0	48
15	London Broil	440	110	12	75	2740	27	0	53
16	Lime-Marinated Steak	340	180	20	95	85	4	0	35
16	Pepper Steak	480	210	24	145	760	10	2	54
17	All-Day Slow-Cooker Beef	320	190	21	85	480	8	1	25
18	Beef Stroganoff	430	110	12	70	710	49	3	29
18	Polish Delight	530	270	30	100	1720	38	4	30
19	Chili Cheese Tater Tot Casserole	570	200	23	75	1400	60	9	40
20	Lentil Beef Casserole	570	40	4.5	60	2680	86	13	51
20	Mexican Beef and Rice	470	80	8	50	730	73	4	25
21	Shepherd's Pie	510	220	24	110	650	37	3	37
21	Spaghetti Pie	720	400	44	190	1500	36	2	50
22	Inside-Out Ravioli	520	200	22	110	900	50	5	31
23	Stuffed Cabbage	240	90	10	100	500	17	3	21
24	Stuffed Green Peppers	220	40	4.5	50	360	21	2	23
25	Upside-Down Pizza Casserole	720	320	35	125	1370	49	2	48
26	Chili	130	70	7	10	570	14	2	5
26	Taco Soup	90	15	2	20	550	11	2	9
27	Pepper Pot Soup	350	90	10	100	630	39	3	26
28	Taco Salad	190	50	6	15	270	27	4	10
28	Chili Sauce for Hot Dogs	150	50	6	40	810	18	2	10
31	Pork Tenderloin	270	140	15	20	170	27	3	8
32	Herbed Pork Roast	360	150	17	110	1710	7	1	44
33	Pork Casserole Milano	480	260	29	50	1280	39	2	15
34	Suwannee County Pork Chops	270	150	17	55	650	11	3	18
34	Down South Barbecue	880	320	36	255	1030	38	3	95
35	Kumquat Chicken	530	280	31	155	1030	19	4	40
36	Beef Baked Chicken	470	290	32	150	980	6	0	36
36	Cheesy Baked Chicken	670	380	42	175	980	24	2	46
37	Oven-Fried Mexican Chicken	310	160	18	90	240	14	1	25

Nutritional Profiles

Pg. #	Recipe Title (Approx Per Serving)	Cal	Cal from Fat	T Fat (g)	Chol (mg)	Sod (mg)	Carbo (g)	Fiber (g)	Prot (g)
38	Oven-Fried Chicken	980	540	60	320	2120	32	1	74
38	Chicken Fantastic	690	340	37	110	1080	59	0	30
39	Linda's Favorite Chicken	680	380	42	215	380	17	1	61
39	Tangy Baked Chicken	410	210	23	115	1050	22	0	29
40	Chinese Chicken with Peppers and Onions	250	140	16	30	1000	16	2	13
40	Chicken Potpie	730	340	38	225	2310	47	7	47
41	Italian Chicken	300	190	21	70	780	8	1	21
41	Chicken and Sausage Casserole	500	180	20	85	2210	36	6	46
42	Chicken with Spanish-Style Rice and Tomatoes	550	170	19	70	1230	65	8	31
43	Mexican Chicken and Rice	360	130	15	60	540	37	3	21
43	Hot Chicken Salad	320	200	22	45	1180	16	2	16
44	White Chili	330	100	12	60	270	31	12	27
44	Curried Chicken Salad	580	330	37	60	890	42	2	17
45	Turkey Cheddar Wrap with Spiced Yogurt Dip	290	90	11	35	820	35	3	20
45	Quick Turkey à la King	550	330	37	175	900	14	2	39
46	Wheat Germ Deviled Eggs	230	190	21	225	210	2	0	7
46	Kumquat Gator	300	80	9	0	810	15	5	37
49	Marinated Amberjack	330	140	16	85	135	1	0	44
49	Easy Flounder Fillets	360	140	16	125	870	6	1	48
50	Kumquat Grouper	180	80	6	40	70	8	3	23
50	Kumquat Polenta	210	80	9	10	1280	32	1	3
51	Grouper Parmesan	190	20	2	65	430	7	0	33
51	Festive Mullet	660	350	39	85	990	38	0	33
52	Smoky Salmon Cheese Ball	110	80	9	35	250	1	0	7
52	Fish Chowder	380	130	14	70	970	32	2	30
53	Jambalaya	450	210	23	175	1080	30	2	29
53	Seafood Chowder (Bouillabaisse)	340	120	13	260	790	17	1	36
54	Baked Fish Guamanian Style	150	70	7	40	180	5	0	14
54	Crabby Potatoes	240	110	12	50	500	23	2	9
55	Hot Crab, Red Pepper, and Onion Dip	60	30	3.5	15	110	2	0	5
56	Crab Casserole	410	230	26	145	620	24	2	20
57	Crab and Tomato Quesadillas	600	210	23	95	1530	63	5	33

Nutritional Profiles

Pg. #	Recipe Title (Approx Per Serving)	Cal	Cal from Fat	T Fat (g)	Chol (mg)	Sod (mg)	Carbo (g)	Fiber (g)	Prot (g)
58	Crab Quiche	260	180	21	100	260	5	0	14
58	Crab Meat Quiche	120	70	8	85	270	3	0	10
59	Delectable Oyster Stew	430	300	33	170	1110	17	1	17
59	Baked Scallops with Tomatoes	180	80	9	40	990	6	1	17
60	Shrimp Casserole	430	180	20	130	660	43	3	17
60	Shrimp Pilaf	410	70	8	190	1820	55	2	28
61	Shrimp Macaroni Salad	200	40	4.5	140	850	24	1	16
61	Shrimp and Spinach Pita Pizzas	390	30	3	65	980	50	4	41
62	Shrimply Delicious Quiche	220	140	15	100	870	10	1	10
62	Creamy Seafood Medley	270	130	15	145	850	8	0	24
65	Baked Spinach and Artichoke Dip	130	60	7	15	360	8	1	11
65	Cheese Ring with Strawberry Preserves	290	210	23	40	240	16	1	8
66	Cheese Lover's Pizza Squares	200	50	5	20	560	23	1	15
67	Confetti Quesadillas with Cilantro Yogurt Dip	410	200	22	60	630	32	4	22
68	Grilled Goat Cheese Sandwiches	390	220	24	60	520	27	0	12
68	Choco-Nana Milk Mixer	170	40	4.5	15	240	25	1	9
69	Festive Fruity Flavored Milk	90	10	1.5	10	70	14	0	5
69	Double Pineapple Breakfast Shake	320	5	1	5	120	73	5	11
70	Breakfast Smoothie	230	60	7	10	160	28	3	13
71	Strawberry Yogurt Smoothie	170	10	1	5	90	36	1	6
71	Coffee Punch	130	70	8	30	45	13	0	2
72	Farmer's Casserole	350	180	20	170	540	24	0	19
73	Mexican Egg Casserole	250	160	18	195	430	6	0	17
73	Cheddar Spinach Quiche	170	110	12	85	270	7	1	8
74	Tomato Quiche	340	200	22	150	920	14	1	21
75	French Toast Casserole	330	230	25	245	280	14	0	11
75	Cheese Garlic Biscuits	170	90	10	20	380	16	0	4
76	Baked Pears with Vanilla Yogurt and Granola	230	25	2.5	5	100	51	4	4
77	Flan	470	150	17	185	200	70	0	12
78	Classic Cream Pound Cake	430	180	20	130	135	59	1	5
78	Strawberry Yogurt Shortcake	290	100	11	15	500	44	3	6
85	Curried Pecans	360	340	38	5	140	7	5	4

Nutritional Profiles

Pg. #	Recipe Title (Approx Per Serving)	Cal	Cal from Fat	T Fat (g)	Chol (mg)	Sod (mg)	Carbo (g)	Fiber (g)	Prot (g)
85	Spiced Pecans	360	300	33	20	65	16	4	5
86	Sweet and Salty Pecans	510	400	45	20	440	24	3	5
86	Pecan Pie	370	130	15	70	95	61	1	4
87	Skillet Cookies	200	90	10	30	120	29	2	2
87	Quick-Mex Bean Dip	30	5	0	0	230	4	0	2
88	Spicy Roasted Garlic and Soybean Dip	140	90	10	0	330	7	1	6
89	Suwannee County Black Bean Soup	100	20	2.5	0	230	14	5	5
89	Slow-Cooker Beans and Sausage	450	20	2	0	1980	97	20	22
90	Peanut Butter Squares	270	160	18	30	140	26	1	3
90	Frozen Peanut Butter Pie	450	260	29	25	150	37	1	7
91	Peanut Butter Zebras	100	50	6	10	65	11	0	1
92	Microwave Soy Nut Brittle	130	25	2.5	0	95	24	1	4
92	Barley Casserole	350	180	20	0	1040	38	5	6
93	Corn Fritters	60	15	1.5	25	95	9	0	2
93	Corn Bread Casserole	290	180	20	75	280	21	3	7
94	Corn Bread Dressing	490	210	23	150	1260	49	4	20
94	Grits Casserole	410	300	34	125	1390	12	1	16
95	Walnut Fried Rice	380	180	20	100	240	30	4	21
96	Delicious Stove-Top Rice Pudding	200	35	4	10	50	36	1	5
96	Cuban Bread	340	0	0	0	490	72	3	11
97	Health Bread	270	40	4.5	0	380	50	4	8
98	Kumquat Banana Nut Bread	400	180	21	35	240	53	4	5
98	Mango Nut Bread	340	130	15	45	60	50	2	5
99	Whole Wheat Banana Bread	210	30	3	25	380	43	3	4
99	Whole Wheat Dinner Rolls	200	70	8	15	200	27	4	6
100	Oatmeal Pancakes	320	70	8	105	1220	48	5	15
100	Granola	380	190	22	5	190	40	6	8
103	Microwave Bananas Foster	450	210	23	0	200	52	3	1
104	Blueberry Buckle	280	80	9	35	210	48	2	4
105	Fruit Cobbler	240	10	1	0	170	55	6	5
105	Blueberry Dessert	440	140	15	10	320	73	4	3
106	Blueberry-Filled Dutch Pancake	220	60	7	140	95	36	3	7

Nutritional Profiles

Pg. #	Recipe Title (Approx Per Serving)	Cal	Cal from Fat	T Fat (g)	Chol (mg)	Sod (mg)	Carbo (g)	Fiber (g)	Prot (g)
107	Blueberry Gelatin Salad	320	120	14	35	100	46	2	4
108	Blueberry Pie	400	200	23	40	110	46	2	3
108	Crustless Blueberry Pie	130	25	3	0	20	27	2	2
109	Blueberry Strata	250	120	14	115	150	27	2	7
110	Fresh Berry-Stuffed French Toast with Yogurt Sauce	380	50	5	55	490	71	3	13
111	Calamondin Cake	730	330	37	125	680	94	3	9
112	Crazy Coconut Pie	330	160	18	130	270	37	1	6
112	Strawberry Fig Preserves	90	0	0	0	10	24	1	1
113	Grapefruit Compote in Rosemary Syrup	190	0	0	0	5	48	2	1
114	Kumquat Cake	300	120	14	25	180	43	1	3
115	Kumquat Flan	340	50	6	130	100	66	0	6
116	Lemon Bars	170	60	7	45	40	26	1	3
117	Grandma's Lemon Meringue Pie	210	15	2	45	170	47	0	2
118	Perfect Lemonade	90	0	0	0	0	25	1	0
118	Easy Key Lime Pie	570	220	25	15	310	76	1	7
119	Key Lime Pie	590	260	29	5	370	71	1	7
120	Spicy Mango and Avocado Salsa	200	100	11	0	10	29	3	3
120	Mango Cake	430	190	21	40	400	60	2	6
121	Crystallized Citrus Peel	410	0	0	0	260	111	4	0
121	Orange Juice Cake	420	220	24	75	400	46	1	5
122	Orange Juice Cookies	150	50	6	10	70	25	1	1
122	Citrus Cookies	240	90	9	10	75	38	1	1
123	Papaya and Avocado Salad with Lime	170	120	13	0	60	13	2	1
123	Pineapple Mango Smoothie	240	15	1.5	10	85	53	1	5
124	Escalloped Pineapple	300	140	16	40	290	36	1	6
124	Black Raspberry Cobbler	350	110	13	5	150	57	2	4
125	Strawberry Angel Delight	80	15	2	5	50	15	1	2
125	Frozen Strawberry Dessert	450	210	23	30	90	57	3	4
126	Caramelized Grilled Strawberries and Ice Cream	340	190	22	35	60	35	3	4
126	Strawberry Fruit Smoothie	260	15	1.5	5	75	56	3	6
127	Strawberry Pretzel Salad	430	150	17	15	660	64	2	6
128	Roasted Strawberry and Tomato Soup	670	350	39	60	550	54	6	15

Nutritional Profiles

Pg. #	Recipe Title (Approx Per Serving)	Cal	Cal from Fat	T Fat (g)	Chol (mg)	Sod (mg)	Carbo (g)	Fiber (g)	Prot (g)
128	Depression Cracker Pie	410	170	19	0	105	57	3	4
129	Vanilla-Grilled Lobster	890	550	62	135	910	53	13	33
130	Watermelon Granita-Filled Lime Cups	60	0	0	0	0	17	1	0
130	Watermelon Lemonade	140	0	0	0	10	40	2	1
131	Watermelon and Spinach Salad	140	70	8	0	420	19	2	2
131	Fruited Ice	60	0	0	0	0	15	1	1
132	Tropical Fruit Mold	90	5	0	0	5	21	2	0
135	Herbed Green Beans	45	15	2	5	20	6	3	1
135	Broccoli Salad	250	200	22	130	180	8	2	6
136	Broccoli Raisin Salad	350	280	32	30	270	16	3	4
136	Light Cream of Broccoli Soup	340	140	15	110	980	20	3	32
137	Broccoslaw	360	210	23	0	270	31	5	9
137	Blue Ribbon Coleslaw	90	45	5	5	140	12	2	1
138	Florida Coleslaw	100	0	0	10	470	20	3	6
138	Frozen Coleslaw	250	5	0	0	500	61	3	2
139	Copper Pennies	300	120	14	0	260	42	4	2
139	Garden Waldorf Salad	170	45	5	0	115	25	5	8
140	Cauliflower Salad	220	90	10	20	930	27	2	8
140	Cucumber Salad	160	60	7	25	70	19	1	4
141	Eggplant Casserole	210	130	15	35	480	13	2	9
141	Spring Peas	110	20	2.5	0	160	17	4	6
142	Hot Potato Salad	230	130	15	50	150	23	3	4
142	Hungarian Potato Salad	250	60	7	50	210	42	6	7
143	Make-Ahead Mashed Potatoes	260	120	13	35	260	33	3	8
143	Party Potatoes	410	280	31	65	710	22	2	8
144	Hot and Spicy Potato Soup	330	40	4.5	15	560	60	5	12
145	Whipped Rutabagas au Gratin	300	130	15	95	310	33	6	8
145	Egg and Spinach Salad	390	300	33	200	530	13	2	10
146	Spinach Pie	790	590	65	125	1390	30	7	18
146	Squash Casserole	360	190	21	55	840	31	4	11
147	Acorn Squash Soufflé	260	170	18	95	710	16	2	7
148	Zucchini Relish	25	0	0	0	200	6	0	0

Nutritional Profiles

Pg. #	Recipe Title (Approx Per Serving)	Cal	Cal from Fat	T Fat (g)	Chol (mg)	Sod (mg)	Carbo (g)	Fiber (g)	Prot (g)
149	Zucchini and Carrot Spice Muffins	190	100	12	25	170	20	1	2
149	Zucchini Soufflé	140	80	9	145	1360	5	1	10
150	Zucchini with Walnuts	120	110	12	0	15	2	1	2
150	Sweet Potato Muffins	200	120	13	20	230	18	2	3
151	Sweet Potato Soufflé	430	140	15	30	85	110	9	7
151	Speedy Sweet Potatoes	260	40	4	0	260	56	5	3
152	Bacon and Cherry Tomato Bites	240	210	23	25	260	4	1	3
152	Crostini with Fresh Tomato Basil Topping	70	25	2.5	0	170	9	1	2
153	Citrus-Marinated Tomato Salad over Steak	590	280	32	100	1440	41	4	35
154	Florida Sun and Sea Chef Salad	370	180	20	150	460	21	6	26
154	Tomato Spinach Dip	130	90	10	30	190	5	1	4
155	Tomatoes and Eggs Alfredo	450	320	35	335	950	15	2	17
156	Tomato, Shrimp, and Couscous Salad	340	110	12	120	630	38	4	21
156	Tomato and Squash Tart	120	45	5	60	340	11	2	6
157	Tortilla Pizzas with Roasted Tomatoes	390	180	20	40	480	37	4	16
157	Tropical Gazpacho Soup	100	0	0	0	190	25	2	2
158	Winter Gazpacho Olé	160	30	3.5	0	1030	25	8	8
159	Greek Salad Pitas	440	190	21	10	1090	50	7	15
159	Veggie Christmas Tree	100	70	8	0	125	6	1	3
160	Tuscan Vegetable Lasagna	290	110	13	20	490	29	6	17
161	Veggie Pasta Primavera	260	45	5	15	470	40	5	14
162	Vegetable Spaghetti Bake	370	130	14	5	790	32	4	25

Index

Index

Index

Index

Index

Index

To order additonal books, please send
$25.00 per book plus $5.00 postage and handling to:
Chris Kilbride
Martin County Extension Office
2614 SE Dixie Highway
Stuart, FL 34996
(772) 288-5654

Make checks or money orders payable to FEAFCS.

For credit card orders, please visit our Web site at www.simplyflorida.org.